Let My People Go

Let My People Go!

The Struggle
of the Jewish People
to Return to Israel

By **Tom Hess**

Progressive Vision Washington D.C.

Published by
Progressive Vision
3024 Bladensburg Rd., N.E.
Washington, D.C. 20018
U.S.A.

Typesetting, Jerusalem, Israel
Printed in U.S.A.

Unless otherwise noted, Scripture quotations in this book are from the New International Version, copyright © 1983 by B.B. Kirkbride Bible Co., Inc. and The Zondervan Corporation.

Dedication and Acknowledgements

This book is dedicated to the God of Abraham, Isaac and Jacob, my closest Friend, my Lord and my King. Only by His strong encouragement and grace were we able to complete *Let My People Go*. This book was published in Jerusalem in obedience to Isaiah 2:3 which says the law shall go forth from Zion and the word of the Lord from Jerusalem.

We have had a lot of help from our friends. Marilyn Levar and Dawn Cole each spent hundreds of hours working to help make the publishing of this book possible. Florence Biros and Susan McElroy were a tremendous help in editing. The International Christian Embassy in Jerusalem and Barry Segal International helped considerably in the preparation and publishing.

Last but not least, many of you who stood in the gap interceeding are greatly responsible for this book being published. Only by God's hand and through your ongoing prayers, fastings, warnings and practical help, and those of many others, will the Jewish people be freed from bondage to escape to Israel.

We pray this book will help spark or kindle a little flame that will grow and encourage a massive Aliyah movement from America and other countries to Israel, biblical Zionism and a growing desire among the Jewish people to seek, know, praise and worship the God of Abraham, Isaac and Jacob in their land.

Thanks to all of you, God's mishpachah for the deliverance of Zion, for your past and future labors to help set the captives free.

Tom Hess

Foreword

I have read the incredible manuscript by Tom Hess *Let My People Go* and believe that he has touched upon a vital truth and an area of deep concern. Our Jewish friends must be reassured that there is no hidden agenda in this powerful message. Those of us in the Christian Zionist movement are currently viewing a neo-anti-Semitism sweeping through the Evangelical ranks. Very frankly, if I were a Jewish person, I would take Tom Hess' message very seriously. Having a love for Israel and the Jewish people, it would give me deep pain for some of my Jewish friends to leave these shores and to make Aliyah to Zion. I think, however, that the pain of staying conceivably could be worse. I do recall that the Jews of Germany were saying that it couldn't happen right up until the time of the unleashing of the Holocaust. If we should see a financial collapse in America there will be a search for a scapegoat. The history of Western Civilization demonstrates that the scapegoat usually, if not always, turns out to be the Jew. Christians and Jews alike should read *Let My People Go* and then make knowledgeable and swift decisions. Mr. Hess is to be highly commended for having the courage to produce this important book.

> Dr. David A. Lewis
> Founder of Christians United
> for Israel and former President
> of the National Christian
> Leadership Conference for Israel

Let My People Go addresses a very important point, the return of the American Jewish people to Israel. This book is another prophetic sign that the Messiah is coming soon.

> Steve Lightle
> Author of *Exodus II*

I am deeply impressed by the genuine desire for the well-being of God's people, the Jews, that is behind the words of this book in the heart and person of the author, Tom Hess, whom I have come to know as a man of love and prayer. May God mightily use the words of this book to stir the church into action so that the words of Isaiah may be fulfilled: "Thus says the Lord; Behold, I will lift up my hand *to the Gentiles* and set up my standard to the people and they shall bring your sons in their arms and your daughters shall be carried upon their shoulders." Isaiah 49:22

Jan Willem Van der Hoeven
Jerusalem, Israel
November, 1987

Having read Tom Hess' book on these significant subjects, I want to give testimony to the profound impression it made upon me. Tom has been a friend and colleague for several years. This book is a major challenge. When a word like this comes forth, it is necessary to seek God for His direction. For me this has meant becoming loose to that which would hold me back from an immediate call of God to pick up stakes and go. To have confidence, one must know the call of God for his own heart and life. The timing and response is made in this inner sanctum. This book challenges us to be sure we have the Lord's direction in these last days.

Dan Juster
Potomac, Maryland

Table of Contents

1 The Struggle of the American Jew To Return to Israel

In Isaiah 49:15,16, God says He will not forget the Jewish people, but has engraved them on the palms of His hands and their walls are continually before Him!

> "Then say to Pharoah, 'This is what the Lord says: "Israel is my first-born son, and I told you, 'Let my son go, so he may worship me.' But you refused to let him go; so I will kill your firstborn son." ' "
>
> Exodus 4:22, 23

> "Therefore, say to the Israelites: 'I am the Lord and I will bring you out from under the yoke of the Egyptians. I will free you from being slaves to them and will redeem you with an outstretched arm and with mighty acts of judgment.' "
>
> Exodus 6:6

LET MY PEOPLE GO is written to communicate the deep, continual and abiding love God has for the Jewish people. He says He will not forget them but has engraved them on the palms of His hands and that their walls are continually before Him. It is because of His love that He always warns them of danger and prepares those who are willing to follow Him in His ongoing purposes throughout history.

Today in America as God's purposes in history are moving onward towards Jerusalem, He is again manifesting His love to

1

His Jewish people. He desires to deliver them from the bondages by which the American culture has entangled them. God in His loving-kindness and faithfulness is warning the Jewish people to escape the judgment and plagues coming upon America, and the Western world.

LET MY PEOPLE GO is directed towards the American Jew, however, the message and warning applies to the whole Western world. The decadence of American society has spread throughout the world through the mass media. However, due to the size of the American Jewish community in relation to those of other Western countries, this book is particularly directed toward them. It should be kept in mind though that all sin will be judged and that no culture or society will be exempt.

Just as they were in Egypt, the Jewish people today are in slavery to many false gods in America. Many American Jews and Christians have not been aware that they are enslaved by a materialistic system and consequently have not had a desire to be freed. Plagues and judgment are already coming on the gods of our contemporary society. My prayer is that the American Jewish people become aware of the bondages to these gods and break from them. They must make Aliyah (return) to Israel before greater judgment or plagues come upon America. The Jewish people in America must be freed from this slavery to materialism in all of its forms in order to escape to Israel. This struggle is even greater than it was to leave Europe fifty years ago because of the way the Jewish people have prospered and been blessed even more in America. Christians in America need to fast and pray, as did the city of Nineveh, for God to stay judgment, for a national spiritual awakening and for the Jewish people to come home to Israel.

LET MY PEOPLE GO is written to both the Jewish and Christian people, particularly in America and Israel, to help them perceive how God has used them together in the past and how God's Divine purpose is sovereignly joining them together at this critical time in history. There are obvious difficulties in trying to communicate this message to both communities at the same time because of the different terminology and concepts used by each. While this book attempts to do just that, it offers a unique opportunity for the two communities to dialogue and better understand each other.

While this is a message in love warning the Jewish people to escape the coming judgments on America and follow God's call to Israel, it also shows Christian Zionists how they have helped the Jewish people in the past and should help in this coming return.

LET MY PEOPLE GO was also written out of an alarming vision and growing concern over this stuggle for freedom by the six million Jewish people in America. Though some rationalists aren't inclined to believe in visions, many are recorded in the Bible. The Prophet Joel said:

> "In the last days, I will pour out my Spirit on all men. Your sons and daughters will prophesy, your old men will dream dreams, your young men will see visions. . . ."   Joel 2:28

On March 19th, 1987 God spoke into my spirit that judgment was at the door in America. Then on March 24, 1987 as I was sharing and praying with another brother, I had a vision. It seemed as if eternity was at my feet. Bombs were going off over our heads. In the vision, I reached for the phone to call someone and warn them, but it was too late. Suddenly, I found myself praying against the powers of Communism and Islam. Then eternity seemed to vanish before me. Afterwards a still small voice in my spirit said: "Severe judgments are coming on America soon, but I am holding them back briefly because the Jews have not been adequately warned to return to Israel."

A mandate was given to me by the Lord to "Blow a Trumpet in Zion" and "Sound an Alarm" throughout America in love, warning the Jewish people to immediately return to Israel. Also, I was instructed to encourage the Christian Zionists in America to pray for, to warn and to help the Jewish people return to their promised land.

The months of my life since I received this message have been very difficult. My work has been one of praying for America (co-ordinating a 24-hour prayer watch at steps of the Supreme Court and Capitol buildings and leading prayer teams to Israel and other nations to pray) and editing a newspaper committed to building

3

bridges between Jews and Christians. I have a deep love and appreciation for my homeland, America, and for how she has helped the Jewish people. I am also grateful to the Jewish people and Israel, having benefited greatly from their culture, religion and friendship. I don't know why God gave me this message, since I am neither Jewish nor an expert in these matters. Sharing this word has been a struggle, but I must speak out because of my deep love for the Jewish people.

My concern and burden should in no way be taken as anti-Semitic or as disregard for my Jewish brethren. I reject wholeheartedly the ancient stereotype of the Jew as a materialistic and greedy person. Instead, I am showing how the Gentile nation of America has become materialistic and greedy. Both Jew and Christian are being defiled by the influences in this society. I could just as easily write a book specifically warning the Christians in America to live godly lives and be a light to the world.

My burden, however, is to be a voice crying in the wilderness that the Jewish people should follow the biblical call and return to Israel, even as I now live in Israel. Israel is not a national ghetto as some would accuse me of saying, but as Isaiah 11:12 says; "It will be the banner for the Nations!"

LET MY PEOPLE GO was written to help give progressive vision and hope to the Jewish people. Many Jewish people have not returned to Israel because of a lack of knowledge and vision in regards to the Torah and God's ongoing purposes in history, calling them back to the land.

"Where there is no vision, the people perish."   Proverbs 29:18

(To receive God's vision for the return of the Jewish people, read, pray, and meditate on the 700 scripture verses under Appendix A in this book.) If the Jewish people take these 700 scriptures promising and calling them back to the land of Israel, as seriously as many people take scriptures on prospering materially, God will soon envision them to return with His blessing to their promised land. If they ignore these commands and promises, they may lose what they have and return as refugees or perish in the Diaspora.

LET MY PEOPLE GO was written recognizing the multifaced dimensions of this struggle. We recognize the difficulties in breaking from greed, materialism and other false gods of our American culture. We must embrace the loving God of Abraham, Isaac and Jacob and His biblical call to return to the land of promise. We also recognize the difficult struggle it is to consider breaking one's family, community and cultural ties when they have been settled in a country for decades, or in some instances, generations, in order to return to Israel.

While it is a struggle for Jewish people, young or elderly, it is even more difficult for middle-aged Jewish families who are in the prime of life and have bought a house, established a vocation and have children in school. When the children of Israel left Egypt and Babylon, and more recently when they left Europe, they had to struggle with many of these same difficulties.

Through prayer and determination to follow the call of the God of Israel to the land, we can break from these false gods and overcome these obstacles. The Jews can be present-day Joshuas and Calebs returning to and possessing the land of promise to worship God. Moving to Israel can be difficult because of inevitable tensions and cultural changes to overcome, like dealing with the bureaucracy and red tape in a culture that does things much slower than America. Things like the school system, banking systems or medical systems seeming to be less efficient and the possibility of having to wait up to a year or more to have a phone installed can be an opportunity to develop patience. However, a massive Aliyah movement from America to Israel could create an alternative to challenge the cumbersome Israeli bureaucracy.

The possibility of having fewer luxuries, making considerably less money for the same job, paying very high taxes, and in some cases leaving your family and relatives behind can indeed be a sacrifice! Also, the difficulties of the Arab-Jewish conflicts in the land could stop the Jewish people from returning today.

These are, however, minimal difficulties and sacrifices compared to those Joshua and Caleb and the early pioneers faced. They spent decades in the wilderness and once they arrived, still had to conquer the Canaanites before they could possess the land of promise.

The rebirth and restoration of the land in this century already have been pioneered by David Ben Gurion, Golda Meir and many others. Consequently, we should recognize that the struggle for the American Jews to escape to Israel should be less difficult than at any other time in history. Following God's call to return to the land to worship is the high calling and destiny of the Jewish people. Don't miss your destiny!

LET MY PEOPLE GO echoes a prophetic command to release the Jewish people to the promised land to worship God! It is the command which Moses proclaimed to Pharoah 3,000 years ago. It is the same declaration that must be made today to the god of materialism and other false gods in America who have gripped both Jew and Christian. Moses commanded Pharoah to "LET MY PEOPLE GO, that they may worship God!" Although Wall Street is not the main thing that keeps the Jewish people in America, it exemplifies the system the Jews must break from in order to make Aliya to Israel. We should speak to the god of materialism in America to give up the Jewish people; and to Wall Street and say: "LET MY PEOPLE GO!"

A Jewish lawyer from New York, Shabtai Alboher, who recently made Aliyah, was quoted by the *Jerusalem Post* in an article entitled "Slavery in America": "Jewish people in Israel should also go to the American Embassy in Tel Aviv and speak on behalf of the release of the American Jews, as Moses did to Pharoah, saying: 'LET MY PEOPLE GO!' "

LET MY PEOPLE GO is a loving prayer for the release and return of the Jewish people. We are beginning an International House of Prayer in Jerusalem and also a continuing fast for the release of the American Jews. Other groups will be coming to Jerusalem for a week or two each year to pray. We are establishing this 24-hour Praise and Prayer Watch in Jerusalem where people will be praying around the clock for the return of the Jews, especially from America, but also from Russia and all the nations. We will also praise and pray for the Peace of Jerusalem, the salvation and healing of the nations and the coming of the Messiah. This watch in Jerusalem is based on Isaiah 62:6,7 which says: "I will set watchmen on the walls of Jerusalem who will not remain silent day or night until Jerusalem is established as a praise in the earth." I will be traveling in America warning the Jews to return and helping them in any way possible. If you are interested in being involved in the praise and prayer watch in Jerusalem or joining a continual fast for the return of the Jewish people, please see the information form at the back of this book.

A donation of $15.00 or more per book is encouraged to help the Jews return. *LET MY PEOPLE GO* is available to all Jewish people and Christian Zionists even if they cannot afford a gift to receive it. *LET MY PEOPLE GO* is also available in book stores for $5.95.

Our hope is that as God works through the message of this book and the continual prayers and fastings of His people, a massive Aliyah movement will take place not only from Russia, but also from America and other countries, to Israel.

This book is to say: "Jewish people, you are greatly loved and you are not alone in this struggle. We will struggle together with you in prayer, warning and helping in this return. May you break from the materialistic culture of America and win the struggle to escape to Israel before it is too late. May you return to worship God and enjoy Him forever in your land."

2 Civilizations Warned Before Judgment

Surely the nations are like a drop in a bucket; they are regarded as dust on the scales; he weighs the islands as though they were fine dust. Lebanon is not sufficient for altar fires, nor its animals enough for burnt offerings. Before him all the nations are as nothing; they are regarded by him as worthless and less than nothing.

Isaiah 40:15-17

Do you not know? Have you not heard? Has it not been told you from the beginning? Have you not understood since the earth was founded? He sits enthroned above the circle of the earth, and its people are like grasshoppers. He stretches out the heavens like a canopy, and spreads them out like a tent to live in. He brings princes in naught and reduces the rulers of this world to nothing. No sooner are they planted, no sooner are they sown, no sooner do they take root in the ground, than he blows on them and they wither, and a whirlwind sweeps them away like chaff.

Isaiah 40:21-24

Surely the Lord God will do nothing but he revealeth his secrets unto his servants the prophets.

Amos 3:7 KJV

Eighty-eight major civilizations of man, according to J.D. Unwin, have come and gone since the beginning of time. Each has begun with a strict code of sexual and moral conduct and ended with a demand for complete freedom to express individual passion. Every society that extended sexual permissiveness and materialistic hedonism was soon to perish: the Babylonian, Persian, Roman, Greek and British are a few examples.

The nations have been warned and judged to varying degrees, but all ceased to be the leading civilizations of their time. The downfall of civilizations often precipitated a new era in history in the timetable of God. For example, exactly 40 years (one generation), from the beginning of Jesus' ministry to 70 A.D., Jerusalem was destroyed and God increasingly began working in a revelatory way among the Gentiles.

Today, we are at such a turning point in history, the fortieth year since the rebirth of the nation of Israel. A big question is how much more time the Jewish people have to return. When one looks at the number 40 as it relates to judgment throughout history, it seems as though the Diaspora Jews may currently be living on borrowed time.

God told Jonah that Nineveh would be destroyed in 40 days. The flood lasted 40 days and 40 nights and destroyed the whole world. During the first Exodus, the unbelieving Israelites who despised the promised land missed their destiny and wandered in the desert for 40 years. The law was given to Moses in 40 days but at the end of that 40 days, judgment fell on the camp for their sin.

Before both temples were destroyed, God gave the Jewish people 40 years of grace to rethink their ways. Ezekiel laid on his side for 40 days, one day for each year, bearing the sin of Judah. Then 40 years after the Northern Kingdom of Israel went into exile in Assyria, Jerusalem was destroyed. Forty years after the Sanhedrin moved from the temple to the market place, and 40 years after Jesus warned of coming destruction, the temple and Jerusalem were destroyed. If in the first and second Jewish states God granted 40 years of grace, is it possible the same could be true in the third?

Throughout biblical history, living in the land of Israel meant living in the abundance of God's blessings. Deuteronomy 28:8 says: "The Lord your God will bless you in the Land He is giving you." Yet, 40 years after the rebirth of Israel most of the Diaspora Jews have not heeded God's call to come home. Just how much longer do they have?

In October of 1987, at the beginning of the 40th year on the Hebrew calendar, a few of us were praying in our house of prayer in Jerusalem. Within a few weeks time an earthquake hit Los Angeles and in New York City the stock market fell a record 508 points in one day. These events could be warning signs of coming judgments on America and the Gentile nations.

It seems as if we are approaching the end of the times of the Gentiles and the cloud of Glory is beginning to lift from the civilization in America and is moving again toward Jerusalem. We are coming full circle to where all roads lead back to Jerusalem, the City of the Great King for the final civilization of man!

After 1900 years of being under Gentile rule, Jerusalem and Israel have both been brought back under Jewish rule. Isaiah 11:10 and 12 says:

> In that day the Lord will reach out his hand a second time to reclaim the remnant that is left of his people from Assyria, from Lower Egypt, from Upper Egypt, from Cush, from Elam, from Babylonia, from Hamath and from the islands of the Sea. He will raise a banner for the nations and gather the exiles of Israel; He will assemble the scattered people of Judah from the four quarters of the earth.

As the Jewish people consider the struggle to escape to Israel may they remember that throughout history God has warned civilizations when they have rejected Him to worship other gods. Scripture describes some of these as the gods of materialism (golden calf), sex (fertility goddesses), abortion (child sacrifice to Molech), atheism, or arrogance and pride. Only after warning and a call to repentance does judgment come upon them.

In most instances in history, when major judgments come on civilizations, as many believe could soon happen to America and other Gentile nations, less than 10% of the Jewish people have escaped. The following are some biblical and historical warnings, types of deliverances, responses and judgments:

THE FLOOD — (Noah gave warning) Only Noah and seven others were saved out of the entire world population. The whole world was destroyed by the flood after Noah warned them for

120 years and built an ark for their deliverance.

SODOM AND GOMORRAH — *(Angels gave warning)* Four were saved out of the entire population of Sodom and Gomorrah and one of them was destroyed by becoming a pillar of salt. Angels warned Lot to take his family and anyone else in the city who belonged to him and flee immediately, then God destroyed these wicked cities and people by fire and brimstone from heaven. Fifteen years ago, before abortion was legalized and AIDS was even thought of, Billy Graham said that if God would not destroy America for her sins, He would have to apologize to Sodom and Gomorrah! How much more so now!

1200—1500 B.C. — *(Moses gave warning)* Moses warned the Egyptian Pharoah to let God's people go, but Pharoah pursued the Israelites and was destroyed. This precipitated the downfall of the Egyptian civilization.

862 B.C. — *(Jonah warned)* Jonah told the people of Nineveh that they would be destroyed in 40 days. All the people fasted and prayed and God delayed destruction for more than 100 years.

721 B.C. — *(Hosea and Isaiah warned)* The Northern Kingdom of Israel fell to the Assyrians and the Israelites were scattered throughout Assyria. Hosea and Isaiah, among others, had rebuked Israel's idolatrous and corrupt ways and warned of this destruction.

586 B.C. — *(Jeremiah and Isaiah warned)* Judah and its capital, Jerusalem, surrendered to Babylonian control after Jeremiah's and Isaiah's warning's fell on deaf ears. The Jews were taken into exile to Babylon.

539 B.C. — *(Daniel gave warning)* Babylon was captured in one night when the Persian leader Cyrus stepped into power without a fight. Daniel warned of the end of Babylonian rule when he literally saw the writing on the wall. Only a small percentage were able to flee.

331 B.C. — *(Daniel gave warning)* The Persian Empire, the largest ever seen in the ancient East, fell to Alexander the Great in one decisive battle. Daniel warned of the end of Persian rule.

133 B.C. — *(Daniel gave warning)* The Greek Empire fell to Rome and the Roman Empire united the then known world under their rule. Daniel also warned of the divison and end of the Roman Empire.

70 A.D. — *(Jesus gave warning)* Jesus warned the Jewish people in 33 A.D. of the soon coming destruction of Jerusalem (Matthew 23:37 and Matthew 24:2). Jerusalem was destroyed in 70 A.D. by Titus, the Roman Commander. Some 1.5 million Jewish people were killed according to Josephus.

(God supernaturally gave warning) According to Josephus, God then warned the Jewish people immediately preceding the attack in 70 A.D. by having a sword appear over the City of Jerusalem for about ten days. The first night of the ten days, the Eastern Gate opened supernaturally and 100,000 fled, i.e. only 7-10% of the population left before its destruction.

1300 A.D. — *(Rabbi Nachmanides gave warning)* One hundred years prior to the Inquisition, he said destruction was coming to the Jews of Spain. He not only encouraged Jews throughout Spain to make Aliyah, but led his followers in making Aliyah to Palestine himself!

1920—1944 A.D. — *(Jewish and Christian Zionist Leaders gave warning of the Holocaust)* Rabbis in Europe in the 1920's and 1930's, preceding the Holocaust, were discouraging the Jews from making Aliyah and moving back to their land. However, Vladimir Jabotinsky was going throughout Europe saying: "Liquidate the Diaspora or the Diaspora will liquidate you," and Dr. Max Nordau was saying that only one-third of the Jews would return to the land and the rest would eventually be assimilated or would die in the Diaspora. These and other Zionists were traveling throughout Europe warning the Jews to leave before and during Adolf Hitler's reign of terror because they sensed impending doom. Hardly anyone listened.

Six million Jewish people were destroyed in Germany and Europe. This happened within 40 years after the time Herzl founded the World Zionist Congress and when the Christian Zionist, Rev. William Hechler, began to teach from the Bible that God would soon restore the Nation of Israel. Hechler also warned that an anti-Semitic movement would come and create a longing for the Jews to return to their land.

While nominal, counterfeit Christians were involved in betraying and destroying the Jewish people in Europe, Christian Zionists were helping the Jewish people. Corrie ten Boom is one such Christian who's story is told in the book and film, *THE HIDING PLACE*. Dietrich Bonhoeffer, a famous theologian, was imprisoned and later killed in a plot to try to stop Hitler. Other voices warned of coming tragedy, yet, only approximately 10% or 600,000 Jews left!

Unfortunately, the Jews had few places to go in the 1930's since the State of Israel had not yet been established. After this tragedy, and the death of six million, the State of Israel was born. Out of death, God has brought new life and hope and has given the Jewish people the land of Israel back after almost 2,000 years. Still, only three million out of the total Jewish population of 13 million have followed God's call home.

1970's A.D. — (Jewish and Christian Zionists warned) Zionist leaders encouraged Jews from Iran to escape and make Aliyah to Israel. Some left, but many stayed and now it is very difficult to leave under the reign of Ayatollah Khomeini.

1977—1983 A.D. — (Jacob Timmerman warned) A newspaper editor warned Jewish people of coming Nazi anti-Semitism in Argentina (a Western country in South America). Timmerman encouraged Jewish people to return to Israel but few left. He was put under house arrest and greatly tortured. Virtually no other leaders stood with him. The American Press stated that 30,000 to 40,000 Jews were missing or tortured. Thousands to this day have never been found. Timmerman is another example of God's faithfulness to warn people before calamity. Bruce Singer, who is an Israeli citizen and an American pastor, had also gone throughout Argentina warning the Jewish people to return.

1988 or soon after — Increasing judgment of God on America!

(Will YOU help warn?) As we observe the moral, economical, military and spiritual state of America, we can again see the hand-writing on the wall. America's days are numbered as the leading world power. To whom much has been given, much has been required. We have been weighed in the balance and found wanting as a nation.

Servants of God have been warning of the coming judgments on America for centuries. During the Revoluntionary War, George Washington, the father of our nation, had a vision about the destruction of America before it was even born. This vision is recorded in the Library of Congress. Washington saw the results of the Revolutionary and the Civil Wars and warned of the coming judgment of America in a third war. The following is the third war or peril George Washington saw coming on America.

The Third Peril

Again I heard the mysterious voice saying, "Son of the Republic, look and learn." At this the dark, shadowy angel placed a trumpet to his mouth, and blew three distinct blasts; and taking water from the ocean, he sprinkled it upon Europe, Asia and Africa.

Then my eyes beheld a fearful scene. From each of these continents arose thick black clouds that were soon joined into one. And throughout this mass there gleamed a dark red light by which I saw hordes of armed men. These men, moving with the cloud, marched by land and sailed by sea to America, which was enveloped in the volume of the cloud. And I dimly saw these vast armies devastate the whole country and burn the villages, towns and cities which I had seen springing up.

As my ears listened to the thundering of the cannon, clashing of swords, and the shouts and cries of swords, and the shouts and cries of millions in mortal combat, I again heard the mysterious voice saying, "Son of the Republic, look and learn." When this voice had ceased, the dark shadowy angel placed his trumpet once more to his mouth, and blew a long and fearful blast.

At the beginning of this century, the Christian Zionist, Charles Parham, the father of the Pentecostal movement, warned of judgments coming on America. Referring to James, chapter five, and Washington's vision, Parham stated: "Prophecy states that near the time of the end the nation will become lifted up and forget God and spread itself abroad in power and self-glory. For these things God will devastate the nation and the whole body of the eagle will be burned, as Washington in his vision towards the end of this nation's history saw cities laid waste from coast to coast."

Also, David Wilkerson, author of the book and movie, THE CROSS AND THE SWITCHBLADE, had a vision a few years ago and has been warning of a coming nuclear destruction of America for the same reasons.

Hal Lindsey, author of the book and movie, THE LATE GREAT PLANET EARTH, also has been warning saying: "AMERICA WILL BE DESTROYED BY A NUCLEAR FIRST STRIKE FROM THE SOVIET UNION."

These warnings and many others have been given to America as a whole. God now seems to be giving a specific warning to the Jewish people in America to return to Israel soon to escape the coming judgment and prepare for the great revival coming to the land of Israel.

At this time, most rabbis and spiritual leaders of Jewish people in America are responding as their counterparts did before the Holocaust in Germany and Europe in the 1920's and 1930's. Many are either discouraging Aliyah saying they are American Jews or are not strongly encouraging it because they are building their own movements. Very few are making it a major priority or leading their congregations in massive Aliyah to Israel despite the biblical injunction to return to the land. In Appendix A, 700 verses of scripture are given which either commanded the Jewish people to return to Israel or which contain promises of God's blessings upon His people in this land.

Meanwhile, during the last 40 years, Israeli Jewish leaders, including former prime ministers and Jerusalem Mayor Teddy Kollek, have been strongly encouraging Aliyah. Prime Minister Yitzhak Shamir also spoke out strongly during a recent trip to New York. Orthodox Rabbi Menachem M. Shneerson, of New York City, leader of the Lubavitch Movement, has been encouraging Aliyah and building a house in Israel. If his 100,000 or more faithful disciples accompany him to Israel, it will create quite a stir! He has never been to Israel and his followers say he believes that when he goes he cannot leave, so building a house probably means he is considering a permanent move.

Many other Israeli Zionist envoys have been encouraging and pleading with the Jewish people in the Diaspora including the well-known Bible teacher, Lance Lambert. Jan Willem van der Hoeven from the International Christian Embassy in Jerusalem, Jay Rawlings, Steve Lightle, Merv and Merla Watson and many other Christian Zionists have been warning the Jews to return as well.

The next world war will probably be World War III mentioned in Ezekiel 38 and 39, and also referred to as the Gog and Magog War. It appears that the nations of the U.S.S.R., Ethiopia, Libya, East Germany, Turkey and Iran, together representing the forces of Communism and the Islamic Revolution, may attack and devastate the U.S.A. as implied in George Washington's vision. But according to Ezekiel 39, when they come against little Israel, God Himself will intervene and destroy them. God says He will send fire on Magog and those who live in the coastlands, possibly referring to Russia and America. Little Israel may be devasted but she *shall survive.*

Israel's future is biblically certain. America is not mentioned specifically at all but many believe New York and America are the heart of Babylon, which the book of Revelation says is to be destroyed.

Many Jewish people have believed that Israel's security is in the military and financial support coming from America. The Jewish people need to be warned that while the support of America has in many ways been a blessing in the past, the future support of Israel will increasingly come from God Himself and hopefully from her loyal Christian Zionist friends around the world.

Psalm 20:7 says some trust in chariots, and some in horses, but we trust in the name of the Lord our God! This scripture will become more important and relevant for Israel in the future. She will realize her increasing vulnerability in trusting in America, and her growing need to depend on, and trust in, the God who keeps Israel and neither slumbers nor sleeps (Psalm 121:4).

In 1980, I received a warning when I visited the Berlin Wall and communist museum in East Berlin. The soon projected dates for communism to take over all the countries of the world, including America, were listed in the museum in German. Although I could not understand all of them, the fact that they had specific dates for communist takeover of each nation made me realize that peace talks ultimately can be nothing more than a smoke screen for a growing strategy to take over the world. Also, the fact that Mikhail Gorbachev and the Soviet Union are strongly against Star Wars (S.D.I.) and a shield over America, may be a warning to us that they may want to be able to launch a surprise attack on America.

The Western world should not be caught by surprise because the communists themselves speak openly about their goals. For instance, Dimitry Manuilski, instructor at the Lenin School of Political Warfare in Moscow, stated in 1930 that war to the hilt between communism and capitalism is inevitable. "To win, we shall need the element of surprise. The Western world will have to be put to sleep. So we shall begin by launching the most spectacular peace movement on record. The capitalist countries, stupid and decadent will rejoice to co-operate in their own destruction. They will leap at another chance to be friends. As soon as their guard is down we will smash them with a clenched fist."

> While people are saying, "Peace and safety," destruction will come on them suddenly, as labor pains on a pregnant woman, and they will not escape.   I Thessalonians 5:3

Communism is not the only enemy of the Western world. The Moslem Fundamentalists also are committed to our destruction. Moamar Gadaffi and Ayatola Khomeini, the two radical leaders of the Islamic Revolution are obviously satanically inspired and both have warned that they are committed to the destruction of America. They have clearly stated their intentions to destroy us.

Some, after reading this book, will say God may judge America but they don't think the time is yet. However, it may be sooner than we think. The communists are now launching the most spectacular peace movement on record both in the West and in the East. Don't forget that in every major civilization most people waited too long to prepare to escape and respond for deliverance. Never, to my knowledge, did a falling civilization respond too quickly. Today is the day to hear God's voice and respond to what He has for you. Business as usual in America is over for all who have ears to hear.

God is warning the Jews of America to make an Exodus from the American civilization to Israel very soon. Israel is to be the next and last civilization of man according to prophecy. It is important that the Jewish people leave America before they get caught in a trap and lose their finances in an economic collapse. They then would go home with nothing, or may get caught in a nuclear holocaust. They would miss their destiny in Israel as six million Jewish people did in Europe earlier in this century.

Many Jewish people from Germany and Europe talked about leaving for years before the holocaust. Sadly, most of them were caught up in the simple cares and anxieties of everyday life. They ignored the warnings and missed the purpose of God for them in their generation. May we be thankful for God's continual faithfulness and lovingkindness in that throughout history He warned His people when judgments were coming so they could escape.

As the philosopher Santayana said, "He who does not learn from the lessons of history is doomed to repeat them." May the American Jewish people learn from the failure of past generations to heed the faithful warning, call and commandments of God to escape to Israel and flee the impending judgments on America. May Gog grant a massive Aliyah movement of American Jewish people to break free from the bondage of American materialism and return to the reborn nation of Israel before it is too late. May God call home many faithful Jewish people who as practical Zionists will help restore Israel to its greatest glory!

3 A Warning of Progressive Judgments on America

The judgments of the Lord are true and righteous altogether.
Psalm 19:9 KJV

"Come, O Zion! Escape, you who live in the Daughter of Babylon!"
Zechariah 2:7

A nation from the north will attack her and lay waste her land. No one will live in it; both men and animals will flee away. "In those days, at that time," declares the LORD, "the people of Israel and the people of Judah together will go in tears to seek the Lord their God. They will ask the way to Zion and turn their faces toward it. They will come and bind themselves to the Lord in an everlasting covenant that will not be forgotten." Jeremiah 50:3-5

God's judgment is righteous in that it honors the Holy God of Israel who cannot stand sin and it enables Him to purge away the cancer of decay and sin from a civilization, society or world.

New York and America, which we believe to be the heart of Babylon today, are on the brink of tremendous judgment, some of which has already begun. Unless the Jewish people escape to Israel, they will experience the ever increasing judgment coming upon America in the next few years! If these increasing judgments don't cause the Jewish people to return to Jerusalem soon, there is little hope they will ever return!

Judgment Begins at the Household of God —
(To Christians)

> For it is time for judgment to begin with the family of God; and if
> it begins with us, what will the outcome be for those who do not obey
> the gospel of God? I Peter 4:17

God is judging individuals, ministries and churches. Many adulterous affairs that have been going on over the last ten years have been recently exposed. Pride, arrogance and the false god of mammon that have seduced many in the church are being exposed. The doctrine that the church must become bigger and better is prideful deception. The church of the future will be more underground due to the persecution and coming financial problems in our society.

Jewish People in Cults and Jewish Assimilation —
(To the Jewish People)

Surveys show that up to 50% of those involved in cults in America are Jewish, yet only 2-1/2% of the total American population is Jewish. Also, more than one million Jewish people in America have been assimilated in the last 40 years. On October 20, 1987, the *JERUSALEM POST* said that 25 to 30% of Jews in the U.S. intermarry. The intermarriage rate increased from 6% in 1964 to 14% in 1975 to 23% since 1980. Portions of families in which non-Jewish spouses converted to Judaism declined from 44% in 1971 to 27% in 1975 to 12% since 1980.

Anti-Semitism Is Increasing — (To the Jewish People)

Louis Farrakan said to a radio audience of 10,000 in Washington, D.C., that soon we will be rolling the heads of Jews down the aisles in America! Anti-Semitism is evident and increasing.

Jewish people could become "scapegoats" if there is a financial collapse in America. Blame would particularly be directed to the Director of the Federal Reserve, Alan Greenspan, and many leading economists who are Jewish.

In 1987, anti-Semitic vandalism increased by 17% in America

according to the Anti-Defamation League of B'nai Brith. This was before the Palestinian protests and riots in Israel began which have caused world opinion to turn increasingly against Israel. The Klu Klux Klan, Neo-Nazi Movements, and other anti-Jewish groups are on the rise.

Jews are safer in Israel because they are in control of their own security rather than being at the mercy of others. Psalm 121:4 says: "He that keepeth Israel shall neither slumber nor sleep." KJV

Economic Judgments — (To Christians and Jews)

In less than four years, America has moved from the greatest investing nation to the greatest debtor nation in the world. Also, for the first time, many countries say they will not be able to repay their debts to us. Our national debt has almost tripled in just the first seven years of this decade. Several large companies have put their money in Swiss banks over the last six months. Monetary and financial collapse may be imminent. Isaiah 60 says that the wealth of the nations is to be gathered and brought to Israel. Unless the Jewish people leave soon, they may have to go back as refugees with nothing.

Abortion — (To Christians and Jews)

Over 20 million babies have been killed in the last 14 years in America! Exodus 20:13 says: "Thou shalt not murder" ("kill" — KJV), yet the U.S.A. has the second most liberal abortion laws in the world! There is so much blood on American soil, it's a miracle we have not already been destroyed as a nation! Many secular, reformed and conservative Jews have encouraged abortion despite the fact that the killing of their future generations will affect the future of the Jewish people. There is little difference between child sacrifice in the Old Testament and abortions today.

> For this reason was man created alone, to teach thee that whosoever destroys a single soul of Israel, scripture imputes [guilt] to him as though he had destroyed a complete world; and whosoever preserves a single soul of Israel, scripture ascribes [merit] to him as though he had preserved a complete world.
> Babylonian Talmud Sanhedrin 37 in Mishna

AIDS: A Judgment of God on Immorality —
(To Christians and Jews)

Although many are being infected in innocent ways, the U.S.A. has more people infected with AIDS than any single country in the world. New York is the largest Jewish city in the world. Although few Jewish people have AIDS, the epidemic is spreading in New York (over 1/2 million cases as of March 1987). The possibilities of innocent people in the mainstream of America catching AIDS is growing. David Wilkerson in his newsletter dated August 24, 1987, reported estimates that more than 55 million will die of AIDS over the next ten years (over 1/4 of the population).

Judgment in Politics and Business —
(To Christians and Jews)

Politicians who have been living in adultery or corruption for decades are being exposed. Past Presidents have gotten away with this, but not today! God is judging at this time. Presidential candidate Gary Hart withdrew from the Presidential race as a result. Business leaders are also being exposed, including Ivan Boesky, Mafia leaders, and many others.

Terrorism — (To Christians and Jews)

> Terror will seize them, pain and anguish will grip them; they will writhe like a woman in labor. They will look aghast at each other, their faces aflame.   Isaiah 13:8

In 1987 the Associated Press reported that the F.B.I. averted 200 cases of terrorism in America in 1986. Thousands of Iranian terrorists are already in America and they could strike at any time. Their most likely place to strike is the larger cities where most Jewish people live.

Erratic Weather Conditions —
(To Christians and Jews)

> "There will be signs in the sun, moon and stars. On the earth, nations will be in anguish and perplexity at the roaring and tossing of the sea."
> Luke 21:25, 26

"I will show wonders in the heaven above and signs on the earth below, blood and fire and billows of smoke. The sun will be turned to darkness and the moon to blood before the coming of the great and glorious day of the Lord. . . ."   Acts 2:19, 20

According to these scriptures, there are coming changes in the heavens and the seas. This will affect the health and lives of many people.

Famine — (To Christians and Jews)
No one ever thought there would be severe famine in America, but it may come sooner than we think. Weather conditions could affect the crop cycle and bring this about. Oil shortages also could affect delivery of food to population centers. Revelation 18 describes famine as one result of the fall of Babylon. Matthew 24 speaks of famine. Also, Luke 6:25 says, "Woe to the well-fed for you will go hungry."

Earthquakes — (To Christians and Jews)
More earthquakes shook the world in 1986 than in any other year in history. Seismologists say the earthquake threat is possibly growing and damage potential is greater because of urban expansion. The two major earthquake faults in the world run through the U.S.A. and earthquakes could happen in America at any time (Matthew 24:7). The two most likely places for earthquakes are on the East Coast and West Coast where it happens that most Jewish people live. Hundreds of earthquakes have destroyed many people during the history of America.

Nuclear Attack — A Primary Concern of this Book! (To Christians and Jews)
Hundreds of cities are targeted for nuclear attack by the Soviet Union and could be destroyed in 15 minutes. Most Jewish people live in large cities in the U.S.A., not in the country, and are therefore susceptible to decimation (Isaiah 6:9-13; Revelation 18).

God judged the nation of Israel in 70 A.D. Now He is about to judge America and the Gentile nations. The Jewish people need to return to Israel or they could experience another

Holocaust! It is time for the American Jewish community to make massive Aliyah to Israel before it's too late!

Progressive judgments will come on America in the coming years. Their severity will depend on the degree of repentance in the near future in America. It would take repentance, fasting, prayer and revival like in Nineveh to turn increasing judgments from America. My prayer is that a warning of progressive judgments on America will be taken seriously by the Jewish people.

God's purposes and plans in the earth to bring all the Jewish people home to Israel shall be fulfilled as Ezekiel 39:28 states. The progressive judgments that God is bringing on America are righteous and should be received by the Jewish people as a clear warning from a loving God that it is time to return to the land of Israel. May the Jewish people be like the sons of Issachar and discern the times in which they live and know what they should do! (I Chronicles 12:32).

As the cloud of Glory, in increasing ways, lifts off of America and moves back to Jerusalem, so will God's favor lift off of the Jewish people in America.

Unless the Jewish people heed the loving warning of a righteous God they will probably be greatly devastated or destroyed by the progressive judgments coming on America.

Precious Jewish people, escape the coming judgments on America and possibly another Holocaust. Return to the reborn land of Israel and help restore your nation to its greatest glory ever!

4 The Rebirth and Restoration Of Jerusalem and Israel

Who has ever heard of such a thing? Who has ever seen such things? Can a country be born in a day or a nation be brought forth in a moment? Yet no sooner is Zion in labor than she gives birth to her children.   Isaiah 66:8

Therefore this is what the Sovereign Lord says: "I will now bring Jacob back from captivity and will have compassion on all the people of Israel, and I will be zealous for my holy name. They will forget their shame and all the unfaithfulness they showed toward me when they lived in safety in their land with no one to make them afraid. When I have brought them back from the nations and have gathered them from the countries of their enemies, I will show myself holy through them in the sight of many nations. Then they will know that I am the Lord their God, for though I sent them into exile among the nations, I will gather them to their own land, not leaving any behind. I will no longer hide my face from them, for I will pour out my Spirit on the house of Israel," declares the Sovereign Lord.
                                                        Ezekiel 39:25-29

God initially revealed the Zionist vision to Abraham, and led the Great Patriarch over 4,000 years ago to the land of Canaan and to Jerusalem which later became known as "David's City." In 1967, Jerusalem was restored as the Capital of the Nation of Israel which was reborn in 1948 and is in the process of being restored. Jerusalem will soon become the Messiah's capital not only for Israel, but for the whole world.

> And it shall come to pass in the last days, that the mountain of the Lord's house shall be established in the top of the mountains, and shall be exalted above the hills; and all nations shall flow unto it. And many people shall go and say, "Come ye, and let us go up to the mountain of the Lord, to the house of the God of Jacob; and He will teach us of His ways, and we will walk in His paths"; for out of Zion shall go forth the law, and the word of the Lord from Jerusalem. And He shall judge among the nations, and shall rebuke many peoples; and they shall beat their swords into plowshares, and their spears into pruning hooks; nation shall not lift up sword against nation, neither shall they learn war any more.   Isaiah 2:2-4

The first mention of Jerusalem in the Bible is in Genesis 14:17-24; when Melchizedek, the King of Salem, brought out bread and wine and blessed Abraham, saying: "Blessed be Abram of the most high God, possessor of heaven and earth." Almost every time we take a group of people to Israel and ascend the hills of Jerusalem, we stop and break bread and wine in remembrance of Melchizedek blessing Abraham and we receive God's blessing as spiritual descendants of Abraham.

After Abraham's time, famine struck the land, and Abraham's descendants sojourned in Egypt. It was at that time God gave Moses the vision to lead the first Exodus out of Egypt, gave the Ten Commandments and established the Tabernacle ritual of sacrifice, bringing tremendous blessing not only upon the children of Israel, but upon all the nations of the world. Then Joshua led the Israelites into the land to possess it.

Almost 1,000 years after Abraham, Jerusalem rose to its greatest glory when King David brought the Ark of the Covenant there and the temple was built by Solomon.

The Tabernacle of David established the worship of the Lord, using rams' horns, trumpeters, cymbals, dancers, singers, the playing of lyres and harps. King David danced and celebrated before the God of Israel. David wrote most of the Psalms, which are the best songs in the world to this day!

Then idolatry entered the nation and soon God's judgment

fell. Isaiah warned of this judgment that came through Assyria and then Jeremiah warned of the second blow by the Babylonians.

The second return of the Jews to the land was under the Persian ruler Cyrus. This return brought even greater blessing not only to Israel, but to the whole world. At the end of this time came Jesus' birth and sacrifical death. Then the biblical message was spread throughout the world to the Gentiles.

1948 was another watershed year. Theodore Herzl had prophecied in 1897 that Israel would be formed within 50 years. Exactly 50 years later, after the terrible devastation of the Holocaust, Israel was reborn in 1948. The first page of the *Jerusalem Post* read, "ISRAEL BORN IN A DAY!" (see Appendix B).

Ironically, Andre Gromyko, the former Minister for Foreign Affairs and now President of the Soviet Union, which now has 2-1/2 million Jewish people bound in slavery, was the first to sign the agreement recognizing Israel as a nation.

Not only was Israel re-established as a nation in 1948, but also the United Nations and the World Council of Churches were formed. Dr. Billy Graham, Dr. Bill Bright, Dr. Richard Halverson and many other evangelical and charismatic ministries also began then. David du Plessis, the father of the charismatic movement, said that God had showed him that after Israel became a nation, the charismatic movement would begin. This is exactly what happened. God then began pouring out His Spirit on all flesh, just what the prophet Joel predicted thousands of years ago would happen in the last days!

1967 and the Six-Day War were also a very significant time in history. Jerusalem was brought back under Jewish rule for the first time since 70 A.D. Many Christians see this as the beginning of the fulfillment of Luke 21:24 which states that Jerusalem will be trodden down by the Gentiles until the times of the Gentiles are fulfilled.

I had the privilege of being born in 1948, the same year Israel was reborn and will be 40 years old five days after Israel's 40th birthday. It was not until 1982 when I was praying and studying in Jerusalem during the Feast of Tabernacles, that God lifted the veil from my eyes and I saw His purposes for Israel and how He is going to bring back the Jews from Russia, America and other nations. A tremendous end-time revival mentioned in Ezekiel 37 is to happen in the land of Israel. I knew I would someday live in Jerusalem and spend time praying there and encouraging others to pray for Israel, for the return of the Jews to Israel, for the peace of Jerusalem, the redemption of the nations and the coming of the Messiah.

In honor of the rebirth of Israel, we have sponsored National Celebrations for Israel's Birthday for the last four years in Washington, D.C., and honored various rabbis for building bridges with Christians.

Since 1982, I have had the privilege of being in Jerusalem and Israel 18 times. We have taken many groups of pastors and lay people, Jews and Christians, to tour the land, to celebrate the Feasts of the Lord and to pray for the peace of Jerusalem and the return of the Jews.

Many times we have prayed on the borders of Egypt, Jordan, Syria and Lebanon for the protection of Israel. Many times we have walked around the Old City praying for the peace of Jerusalem and peace between Jew and Arab, and the coming of the Messiah to bring everlasting peace. We have prayed for the Jewish people at synagogues. We have prayed for people in hospitals. We have met with soldiers at army bases and sung and given them gifts, prayed for them and blessed them. We even had the privilege of meeting the President of Israel.

I remember being in Jerusalem when the Ethiopian Jews first returned and we prayed with them during their struggle to be integrated into Israeli society.

We have taken hundreds of boxes of clothes to Israel for the Jewish people. We are planting a grove of trees called "SHALOM JERUSALEM GROVE" in Israel. Many of those on our tours have planted trees, not only in their names, but also in the names of their families and friends. Many have given their blood for the Jewish people. But we have all been blessed far more than we have blessed the Jewish people.

We have been blessed by the love of the Jewish people; by the Bible, the Prophets, the land they have restored. We have been blessed by the heritage we have in our Jewish roots. We have been blessed by the privilege of taking Jews and Christians to modern Israel, by all of our friends and guides in Israel, and by seeing many people come to know God in fuller ways by being in Israel. Seeing the Dead Sea scrolls and the fishing boat recently found in the Sea of Galilee from the time of Jesus blessed us greatly.

We have been blessed by all the beautiful biblical sites; by falafels, by vegetables for breakfast, by St. Peter's fish on the Sea of Galilee. We have been blessed by the beautiful Israeli music and dancing, children dancing at the Wall on Simchat Torah, and by the Sabbath rest when all businesses are closed. We have been blessed by observing Yom Kippur in the land, remembering the blood atonement for our sins and no cars on the roads. The educational museums, the beautiful seas and the desert blossoming like a rose have blessed us as has the God of Israel, the God of Abraham, Isaac and Jacob.

Having been so privileged to witness these blessings we feel a responsibility to help fulfill the Zionist vision.

We have been so blessed by the land of Israel as Christians. One must wonder why the Jewish people, having been given their own nation back after the Holocaust, continue to sing the songs of Zion in the strange lands of Babylon instead of returning to their beautiful land of promise and destiny!

A great day is coming for the Jewish people who escape to Israel from the Gentile nations! In Ezekiel 39:28, 29 God says He will gather them to their own land not leaving any behind. He will no longer hide His face from them for He will pour out His Spirit on the House of Israel.

If the first two returns brought such blessings on the world, how much more will this third return?

> For if the casting away of them be the reconciling of the world, what shall the receiving of them be, but life from the dead?
> Romans 11:15 KJV

The fullness of this third return will bring back the Messiah.

The 20th century truly has been a time of restoration. God began pouring out His Spirit on the Gentiles at the beginning of this century when by His Spirit He gave Theodore Herzl the vision of the restoration of Israel. This move of the Holy Spirit among both Jews and Christians has continued in increasing waves from the turn of the century until our time.

The greatest day of restoration still is in the future as millions of Jews return from the Soviet Union, America and other nations and as God pours out His Spirit upon the Jewish people in the land.

The first edition of this book was printed two days before the rioting began in Israel in December of 1987. Many American Jews and Jews from other nations have been very critical of how the Israelis have handled the situation. Admittably, they made mistakes, however, if the American Jews and others in "free" Western nations had followed God's call home to Israel over the last 40 years, these problems would not exist as they do today! If the American Jews want to help the situation in Israel, they should stop pointing the finger and make Aliyah.

If the land of Israel was flourishing and overflowing with Jewish people, as the Prophets say it will be, the world would look on and say there is not even enough room for the Jews who just came through the holocaust. But only a fraction of the promised land is inhabited by the Jewish people while the remainder is considered "occupied territory" by world opinion — a territory belonging to others. If the American and Russian Jews had returned and began possessing the land God had given them, then these problems would not have arisen. May they return soon before more problems arise.

David Ben Gurion said, that by developing the Negev, Israel could be a country the population size of Belgium, according to Gershon Rivlin, an expert on Ben Gurion. Belgium, geographically the size of Israel, had 10 million people when he made the statement:

> "I will surely gather all of you, O Jacob; I will surely bring together the remnant of Israel. I will bring them together like sheep in a pen, like a flock in its pasture; the place will throng with people."
>
> Micah 2:12

> "The one who breaks open the way will go before them; they will
> break through the gate and go out."   Micah 2:13

In 1987 Israel still has less than five million of the 10 million
people Ben Gurion envisioned in the Land. Room still remains
for millions to return.

Our concern is for those Jews in America who refuse to return
to Israel. While God says He will not leave any behind (Ezekiel
39:28, 29), He never says they will all return, but that all of a
remnant will return. According to this scripture, it seems that the
Jewish people will either return to the land or die in the Diaspora.

As increasing judgments come on the Gentile nations,
especially America, millions could be killed there unless they return
soon. There are over 700 scriptures (see Appendix A) calling the
Jewish people to return to Israel, and I have yet to find any scriptures that specifically tell the Jewish people to remain in the
Diaspora!

The second paragraph of the Sh'ma says:

> And if you will obey my *mitzvot* which I command you this day, to
> love *Adonai,* your God, and to serve Him with all your heart and
> with all your soul, He will give the rain for YOUR LAND in its
> season. . . . Take heed lest . . . you perish quickly off THE GOOD
> LAND which *Adonai* gives you. You shall therefore lay up these
> words of Mine in your heart. . . . And you shall write them upon the
> doorposts of your house and upon your gates, that your days and
> the days of your children may be multiplied IN THE LAND which
> *Adonai* swore to your fathers to give them, as long as the heavens
> are above the earth.   Deuteronomy 11:13-21

In the words of Dr. David H. Stern: "The Sh'ma is not just
for *mezuzot* on doorposts and gates in New York, Philadelphia,
Washington and Los Angeles. It is a ringing encouragement to
move on to *Eretz Yisrael.* Put your *mezuzah* on a doorpost in
Jerusalem, Tel-Aviv, Beersheva or Afula! Return from exile to
THE LAND *which* God *gave to your fathers* . . . and to you! Plan
your *ALIYAH* now!"

Jewish people, escape to Israel before increasing judgments
come on America. After thousands of years of persecution it has
been a blessing to hide under the security blanket of American

society but the blanket is being pulled off. God has never allowed you to be a completely assimilated people. God wants to regather you again from America. American Jews: Don't miss your destiny . . . discern the times in which you live! Return to Israel and participate in the physical and spiritual restoration of all things in Israel.

Although Israel will also go through many difficult days in the future, her greatest days are still to come; days of greater glory than in King David's time, days that will bring the latter rain of the Holy Spirit that will be greater than the early rain. The days are approaching that will bring the coming of the Messiah! Obey the commandments of your God and return to Israel soon to participate in the natural and spiritual restoration of your promised land, your everlasting possession in the God of Israel.

5 Soviet Jews Bound by Communism

"Do not be afraid, for I am with you; I will bring your children from the East and gather you from the West. I will say to the North, 'Give them up!' and to the South, 'Do not hold them back,' Bring my sons from afar and my daughters from the ends of the earth — everyone who is called by my name, whom I created for my glory, whom I formed and made. . . ." All the nations gather together and the peoples assemble. Which of them foretold this and proclaimed to us the former things? Let them bring in their witnesses to prove they were right, so that others may hear and say, "It is true. You are my witnesses," declares the Lord, "and my servant whom I have chosen, so that you may know and believe me and understand that I am he. Before me no god was formed, nor will there be one after me. I, even I, am the Lord, and apart from me there is no Savior. I have revealed and saved and proclaimed — I, and not some foreign god among you. You are my witnesses," declares the Lord, "that I am God."
Isaiah 43:5-7, 9-12

"Forget the former things; do not dwell on the past. See, I am doing a new thing! Now it springs up; do you not perceive it? I am making a way in the desert and streams in the wasteland. . . ."
Isaiah 43:18, 19

"However, the days are coming," declares the Lord, "when men will no longer say, 'as surely as the Lord lives, who brought the Israelites up out of Egypt,' but they will say, 'As surely as the Lord lives, who brought the Israelites up out of the land of the north and out of all the countries where he had banished them.' For I will restore them to the land I gave their forefathers."   Jeremiah 16:14, 15

Almighty God is about to do a new thing that may make the former Exodus out of Egypt look insignificant! The Pharoah of the Soviet Union will be forced to give up millions of Jewish people to return to Israel when God says to the North, "Give them up!" This may happen very soon!

In 1982, I had the privilege of meeting in Jerusalem with Steve Lightle and seven other people from different parts of Europe who had visions and were preparing for the Exodus of the Jews from Russia. (Steve Lightle has written a book on the Exodus of the Jews out of the U.S.S.R., called *EXODUS II*.) Ever since that day, it was evident God was planning to bring the Jewish people out of the Soviet Union soon. *EXODUS II* was going to become a reality and the burden of their deliverance became mine also.

In October of 1985, we led a prayer team of Jews and Christians to Egypt and Israel. On the top of Mount Sinai, where Moses prayed and God gave the vision to deliver the Jewish people out of Egypt, we prayed and called the Jews back to Israel. The prophetic message received at that time was: "You are reliving the Exodus of the past, now I am calling you to go to Russia and America to prepare the way for the Exodus of the future!" That message inspired our first Prayer Team to tour Russia in October of 1986. It was a major undertaking. Thirty-eight people went, both Jew and Christian. Visas were not granted to us by the Soviet Embassy here in Washington, D.C., until 18 hours before we departed and only after much intercessory prayer.

God's presence and Holy Spirit greatly encompassed us on this prayer tour. One church had 24-hour daily prayer watches during the whole trip. Dozens of churches and hundreds of individuals also prayed feverently.

Our entrance to Leningrad was on a cold night. It was raining and hailing. As soon as we got off the plane and onto the bus, KGB guards abruptly faced us and silently seemed to be saying, "We welcome you to this no-nonsense, humanistic, atheistic

34

country," with a cold chilling stare!

First, we visited the Hermitage museum in Leningrad, one of the best art museums in the world. Ironically it was filled with Jewish and Christian art from the 17th to the 19th centuries. Then, we met with a number of different Refuseniks (Jews who have lost their jobs because of applying for emigration to Israel). They shared with us how they were being mistreated and persecuted because of their desire to return to Israel. They were very grateful for our prayers, encouragement and gifts. Some have subsequently been released to return to Israel. I spent most of a night with Valeri Barinov, a Christian musician in Leningrad, who has led hundreds, perhaps thousands, of Gentiles to the Lord in Leningrad. (Not only Jews, but also Christians are being persecuted in the U.S.S.R.!) Every year the Soviets moved him from one job to another because he led so many to know God, including KGB agents. Eventually he was put in jail for three years and badly persecuted, including having his ribs broken for talking about God, but this did not stop him. He probably led one hundred people to the Lord in prison where he started a church. The KGB was so frustrated that they released him from prison a few weeks before we met him. He is the most fearless person I have ever met. He released the Trumpet Call to the world and has been written up in *Rolling Stone* magazine and other places.

On Yom Kippur, we visited the Synagogue in Moscow and gave clothing and Bibles to the Jewish people. We also did a Jericho march around the Kremlin and Red Square, like Joshua did around Jericho, praying for the release of the Jews. We were told later that the Jews are in one prison that is literally under the Kremlin.

We also sang, "O Come Let Us Adore Him," in front of KGB agents in a museum that was once the Church of the Annunciation of the birth of Jesus. There were beautiful pictures of Jesus' birth at this museum right in the heart of the Kremlin.

Our time in the Soviet Union was during the three days of the Summit meeting with President Reagan and Secretary General Gorbachov in Iceland. This opened up many doors of conversation through which many lives were eternally changed.

Progressing directly from Moscow to Jerusalem, we helped prepare "The Highway of Deliverance," by praying through

Europe on our way back to the promised land. From the Free Russian Church in Jerusalem on the Mount of Olives; we commanded the North, in the name of the God of Israel, to give up the Jews, as Isaiah 43:6 says, and we called them back to Israel. Within a few days after this prayer mission to Russia the communists agreed to release 12,000 Jews to Israel within a year.

Our second prayer tour to Russia took place in March and April of 1987, just a few days after my traumatic vision related previously in the first chapter. After this vision of bombs going off over my head and America being attacked by the forces of Communism and Islam, we left on this mission knowing we were on a divine call. In Moscow, God opened the book of Daniel and Revelation to us. Daniel, Chapter 10, shows how the Archangel Michael helped Daniel understand God's plan for the Jewish people at the end of the age. God showed us from Daniel 12:1 that Michael was arising to deliver the Jewish people out of the Soviet Union. A remarkable "coincidence" is that one of the major church museums in the Kremlin is called "The Church of Michael the Archangel," who is the angel traditionally associated with the protection of the Jews. We prayed in the church for the Jews' deliverance and enjoyed the beautiful biblical art! We also saw that Michael, the Archangel arose, that he would take on Lucifer as mentioned in Revelation 12:6-8 and that there would be war in heaven and Lucifer would be cast out of the second heaven upon the earth, embody the False-Messiah and a great war would be manifested in the earth, beginning the Great Tribulation.

Sensing it was time for Michael the Archangel to arise, and for the Jews to be released as Daniel 12:1 states, we did another Jericho march around the Kremlin. We prayed asking God to release Michael and the other angels under him to arise and deliver the Jews back to Israel from both the U.S.S.R. and the U.S.A. and other countries. We also visited the atheistic museum in Leningrad. This building is an old church building that was converted into a museum. The bottom floor consists of an extremely large statue of a nude man, representing the god of Communism, with little cherubs or devils around him. The central focus is a picture of Lenin with all the religions and cultures of the world being subjugated by Communism. The cross is broken in two. The

American, British, Swiss and other flags are torn in two and the hammer and sickle triumph over the world. We did another Jericho march around the atheistic museum, and with the Sword of the Spirit laid the axe to the spiritual root of Communism in the very city where Lenin instituted this demonic ideology in 1917. (1987 was the 70th anniversary of the communist revolution!)

As of this writing, some of the Refuseniks that people in our prayer tour met with have been released including Vladmir Slepak and Michial Zivin. Margaret Thatcher was very instrumental in the release of Valeri Barinov who along with his family spent a day praying with us at our House of Prayer in Jerusalem in early 1988.

God will increasingly bring plagues on humanistic, atheistic Communism, and hopefully, millions of Soviet Jews will be set free. Shabtai Alboher said in the *Jerusalem Post,* "Soviet Jewish activists, unencumbered by the culture and distorted values of the American exile today are truly expressing the authentic Jewish spirit much more than the American Jews." Eight times as many Soviet Jews per million population made Aliyah than American Jews over the last 40 years.

While I believe strongly in the coming Exodus of the Jews from the Soviet Union and have been working towards that end, I concur with Anatoly Scharansky, a leading Soviet Refusenik. During his visit to Washington, D.C., a few months after he was released from prision in Russia to make Aliyah to Israel, Scharansky said, "The enemies in the U.S.A. are much more subtle, deceptive and hard to recognize."

The god of materialism in the U.S.A. has a stronger hold on the Jewish people than the god of atheism has in the U.S.S.R. God says He wants to bring the Jews out of not only the land of the North, but all nations. This means His biggest task is getting them back from the U.S.A. to Israel. Many believe the Exodus from Russia and America will be more spectacular than out of Egypt. If necessary, God will bring plagues and judgments not only on the Pharaoh of atheistic Communism in Russia, but also on the god of materialism in the Babylon of America to "GIVE UP" the Jewish people!

More of the Jews coming out of the U.S.S.R. to go to Israel

end up being seduced by the god of mammon, and coming to America, than following God's call back to Israel. Even though eight times as many Soviet Jews go to Israel than American Jews, the *Jerusalem Post* reported on August 27th, that in 1987 some 80% of the Soviet Jews that were given exit visas to Israel so far that year went to America. Unless American Jews set an example by breaking free from materialism in following the commandments of God to make Aliyah to Israel and become practicing Zionists, the Soviet Jews will continue to follow the god of materialism and luxury to America rather than following their call, deliverance and destiny to Zion!

6 New York and America The Heart of Babylon

By the rivers of Babylon, there we sat down, yea, we wept, when we remembered Zion. We hung our harps upon the willows in the midst thereof. For there they that carried us away captive required of us a song; and they that wasted us required of us mirth, saying, "Sing us one of the songs of Zion." How shall we sing the Lord's song in a foreign land? If I forget thee, O Jerusalem, let my right hand forget her cunning. If I prefer not Jerusalem above my chief joy. Remember, O Lord, the children of Edom in the day of Jerusalem, who said, "Raze it, raze it, even to the foundation thereof." O Daughter of Babylon, who art to be destroyed; happy shall he be, that rewardeth thee as thou hast served us. Happy shall he be, that taketh and dasheth thy little ones against the stones.

Psalm 137 KJV

"Come out of her, my people! Run for your lives! Run from the fierce anger of the LORD. . . . You who have escaped the sword, leave and do not linger! Remember the LORD in a distant land, and think on Jerusalem."   Jer. 51:45, 50

Just as in ancient times when the Israelites wept by the rivers of Babylon and promised never to forget Jerusalem, so today the Jewish people are sitting by a river of Babylon in America. The difference is that they are not yet weeping to return to Jerusalem today.

Ezekiel 17:1-10 is an allegory about two great eagles. The first eagle depicts ancient Babylon and the second eagle though historically was Egypt, is applicable to the end-time Daughter of Babylon, who we believe to be New York and America. Ezekiel tells how the first eagle, the King of Babylon, came to Jerusalem and took King Jehoiachin captive. Daniel and thousands of others of the Jewish people were physically taken captive to Babylon by Nebuchadnezzar. II Kings Chapter 24, says all were taken except the poorest people. The Jews were greatly blessed during their 70 years in Babylonian captivity and accumulated great wealth. Ezekiel tells how the vine of Israel grew and became a spreading vine of low stature, whose branches turned toward this eagle alone, and the vine prospered. Then:

> There was also another great eagle with great wings and many feathers; and beyond, this vine did bend its roots toward him, and shot forth its branches toward him, that he might water it by the furrows of its plantation. It was planted in a good soil by great waters, that it might bring forth branches and that it might bear fruit, that it might be a well-favored vine. Say thou, thus saith the Lord God: "Shall it prosper? Shall he not pull up its roots, and cut off its fruit, that it wither? It shall wither in all the leaves of its spring, even without great power or many people to pluck it up by its roots. Yea, behold, being planted, shall it prosper? Shall it not utterly wither, when the east wind strikes it — wither away in the plot where it grew?"
> Ezekiel 17:7-10 KJV

In verse 9, God says,

> Will it thrive? Will it not be uprooted and stripped of its fruit so that it withers? All of its new growth will wither. It will not take a strong arm or many people to pull it up by its roots. Even if it's transplanted will it thrive? Will it not wither completely when the east wind strikes it — wither away in the plot where it grew!

An east wind is a definite sovereign act of Almighty God. Ezekiel 19:12 gives another example of an east wind:

> But it was uprooted in fury and thrown to the grown. The east wind made it shrivel, it was stripped of its fruit; its strong branches withered and fire consumed them.
> Ezekiel 19:12

These insights are partially taken from Dr. Robert Hooley,

former pastor of Faith Bible Church in Denver, Colorado.

God's purpose is for His people to return to Israel; but those who refuse could be caught in the fire of another Holocaust! Yet, it is worth mentioning, more Jewish people left Israel for America than came to Israel from America in 1987.

The assimilation of Jewish people into Gentile culture and the number joining religious cults are just a few of the judgments of the east wind that are already affecting the future of the Jewish community in America. Although they have not yet caused substantial Jewish emigration to Jerusalem, other judgments are coming very soon which will cause the Jewish people to weep and many to return to Israel if it's not too late.

The historic city of Babylon was famous for its wealth and hedonism. The center of life was focused around man, his rights, his pleasures, his ease and wealth and comfort.

The book of Revelation in Chapters 17 and 18 describes Babylon in the last days in a similar manner. Babylon is described as a geographic city, although it also seems to be a worldwide system and in a broader sense, consists of the evil cities of the world.

The two characteristics that most exemplify Babylon in Revelation are materialism and hedonism. New York is not only the leading city in the world in regards to money and materialism (with the World Money Market centered there), but also may be the leading city in the world in regard to perversion and hedonism. The *New York Times* stated in March 1987 that more than a half million people there are already infected with the AIDS virus. Doctors say up to five million could be infected by 1992 in New York alone!

New York and America are the heart of Babylon today. New York and America have become a man-centered society. We are referred to as the "me" generation; man, self, materialism, hedonism, ease and luxury are worshipped sooner than the true God of Israel (just as in Babylon of old). We have spent hundreds of hours praying for New York City, praying that revival and salvation come to the city, and that the Jews leave before destruction comes.

Revelation 18 says that "the kings of the earth committed adultery with Babylon and the merchants of the earth grew rich from her excessive luxuries." God gave her torture and grief for the equivalency of luxury and glory she gave herself. "In her heart she boasts, 'I sit as a queen, I am not a widow and I will never mourn.' " Some believe the Fourth of July celebration in New York in 1986, with all the drunkenness, materialism, sensuality and boasting in "The Queen," the Statue of Liberty, exemplified Babylon moving towards the fulness of her cup and becoming ripe for judgment. We live as if the rest of the world and its troubles cannot affect us. "In one day her plagues will overtake her; death, mourning, famine. She will be consumed by fire . . . for mighty is the Lord God who judges her! When the kings of the earth who committed adultery with her and shared her luxury see the smoke of her burning, they will weep and mourn over her. 'Woe, woe, O great city of power, in one hour your doom has come!' " This judgment on Babylon (New York) and America will come soon.

The United Nations is centered in New York. The nations within the United Nations have allowed the killing of more than 100 million of their own citizens by various means. This has happened through oppressive regimes in countries such as Russia, China, Cuba and others and, in addition, approximately one billion abortions have been performed worldwide.

Although the United Nations received Israel as a member and recognized its existence in 1948, Kurt Waldheim was U.N. General Secretary for ten years. Evidence points to Waldheim having possibly been a Nazi officer. Man formed the United Nations to try to bring together the nations of the world, but this has not succeeded. In fact, the United Nations has generally proven to be very anti-Israel over the past 40 years.

When we led a prayer team in New York to pray at the United Nations, we saw the sign that has the famous scripture from Isaiah 2 on it which reads:

> They shall beat their swords into plowshares, and their spears into pruning hooks; nation shall not lift up sword against nation, neither shall they learn war any more.   Isaiah 2:4 KJV

This is a noble banner with a noble aim, but God's plan shows that world peace will proceed from Jerusalem not New York. Isaiah 2:3 states:

For out of Zion shall go forth the Law, and the word of the Lord from
Jerusalem.   KJV

God will judge between the nations and settle disputes for
many peoples. Isaiah 11 also says that Israel is a banner for the
nations, not New York!

Unity, world redemption and restoration of the people of God
are not going to spring from New York (Babylon), but from
Jerusalem (Psalm 48:2).

The Messiah is not coming to New York; but like Zechariah
14 says, He will come to Jerusalem and stand upon the Mount
of Olives.

Why are there more Jews in New York than any city in the
world and more Jews in America than any nation in the world?
Despite a Holocaust that killed six million Jewish people in a
foreign land, and despite the rebirth of their homeland, Israel,
just 40 years ago, they refuse to leave America. Historically, as
today, they found it easier and more comfortable to live in Babylon
than to rebuild in a war-torn land. Today they are more committed
to materialism and ease in Babylon and being an American Jew
than God's call for them to return to their end-time destiny in
the land of Israel. Secular and Torah-based Jewish people alike
in America are not taking seriously some 700 scriptures calling
the Jewish people to escape the Babylon of America and other
nations and return to the land of Israel.

Shabtai Alboher said in the *Jerusalem Post,* "When former
prisoner of Zion Yosef Mendelevich was caught trying to hijack
a plane from Leningrad to Israel, the Soviets offered him a choice;
death or life on the condition that he renounce his Zionism and
allegiance to the Jewish state. In prison, they tried to persuade
him by convincing him that he was really a Russian at heart.
'You're one of us,' they told him, 'We speak the same language,
grew up together, shared the same experiences. What makes you
think you're any different from us?' At this point Mendelevich
realized that the greatest threat to his life and freedom was not
imprisonment, but the possibility of denying his Jewish identity.
He asked himself a question that most American Jews will not

yet consider posing: 'Would my life have value if I cannot be myself? That is if I can't express my Jewishness!' Mendelevich refused to recant and today lives as a free man in Jerusalem."

The Jewish people in America, other nations and even some in Israel seem to have in many ways lost their true sense of purpose, uniqueness, identity and destiny as a people. Their Jewish national identity falls victim to the lure of luxury in the U.S. Their values are such that they prefer a Mercedes in America to a modest apartment in Jerusalem. They seem to have forgotten their high calling to be the head and not the tail among the nations. Many religious and non-religious Jewish people in America and even some in Israel have been seduced by (and find themselves trying to emulate) the secular materialist priorities of the Babylon of America rather than fulfilling their destiny in God by leading the way in righteousness in Israel as a light to the nations. This is exemplified by the fact that over the last 40 years, 300,000 Jews have left Israel for America, while only 60,000 have made Aliyah to Israel from America. It seems that the only things that will cause massive Aliyah movements from America are judgment or spiritual revival. Increased anti-Semitism in America, an economic crash, and other judgments on America could spur Aliyah.*

A more preferable and just as effective means would be for biblically based revival movements such as the "teshuvah" of the 1960's to break out within all branches of Judaism. When the Jewish people begin to respond to their biblical call as Israelites to make Aliyah and to love their God and Zion they will turn from serving the gods of materialism and luxury in Babylon as "American" Jews. Hopefully, it will be revival, not judgment that will bring the American Jews home to Israel. Psalm 137:8, listed at the beginning of this chapter, says the Daughter of Babylon is to be destroyed. I believe God is speaking Revelation 18:4 to the Jewish people in New York and America:

"Come out of her [Babylon — U.S.A.] my people so that you will not share in her sins, so you will not receive any of her plagues."
KJV

---

*This manuscript was prepared before "Black Monday" of October, 1987 when the stock market fell 508 points.

Zechariah 2:7 says:

"Deliver thyself, O Zion, that dwellest with the Daughters of Babylon:"
KJV

God is beckoning and calling the Jews home to Israel. Will they respond to God's wooing, begin weeping for Jerusalem again, and return to Israel . . . or be caught in another Holocaust?

7 American Jews: Bound by Materialism

Those who cling to worthless idols forfeit the grace that could be theirs.
                                                                Jonah 2:8

Shake off your dust; rise up, sit enthroned, O Jerusalem. Free yourself from the chains on your neck, O captive Daughter of Zion. For this is what the Lord says: "You were sold for nothing, and without money you will be redeemed."   Isaiah 52:2, 3

"Arise, shine, for your light has come, and the glory of the Lord rises upon you. See, darkness covers the earth and thick darkness is over the peoples, but the Lord rises upon you and His glory appears over you. Nations will come to your Light, and kings to the brightness of your dawn. Lift up your eyes and look about you: All assemble and come to you, your sons come from afar, and your daughters are carried on the arm. Then you will look and be radiant, your heart will throb and swell with joy; the wealth on the seas will be brought to you, to you the riches of the nations will come. Herds of camels will cover your land, young camels of Midian and Ephan. And all from Sheba will come, bearing gold and incense and proclaiming the praise of the Lord. All Kedar's flocks will be gathered to you, the rams of Nebaioth will serve you; they will be accepted as offerings on my altar, and I will adorn my glorious temple. Who are these that fly along like clouds, like doves to their nests? Surely the islands look to me; in the lead are the ships of Tarshish, bringing your sons from afar, with their silver and gold, to the honor of the Lord your God, the Holy One of Israel, for he has endowed you with splendor. Foreigners will rebuild your walls, and their kings will serve you. Though in anger I struck you, in favor I will show you compassion. Your gates will always stand open, they will never be shut, day or night, so that men may bring you the wealth of the nations — their kings led in triumphal procession. For the nation or kingdom that will not serve you will perish; it will be utterly ruined. The glory of Lebanon will come to you, the pine, the fir and the cypress together, to adorn the place of my sanctuary; and I will glorify the place of my feet. The sons of your oppressors will come bowing before you; all who despise you will bow down at your feet and will call you the City of the Lord, Zion of the Holy One of Israel."   Isaiah 60:1-14

The wealth of all the surrounding nations will be collected — great quantities of gold and silver and clothing.   Zechariah 14:14

It is time for the Jewish people in America to set an example for the Soviet Jews. It is time to break from the god of materialism in America and to take whatever wealth they have in America back to Israel as they did from Egypt and Babylon centuries ago!

The sterotype of "rich American Jews" is a misconception. Most are average in income and as recently as 1986, 800,000 Jews were living below the proverty level. However the Jewish people in America are still just as bound emotionally and economically as the Jewish people in Russia are bound physically in their country.

Historically the Jewish people in Egypt were physically bound under slavery and could not prosper, while in Babylon they prospered and were bound under the influence of materialism. Today Secularism is being manifested through both the face of Communism in the U.S.S.R. and the face of materialism in America. As many of them did not want to leave the Disapora when God told them to throughout history, the same is true in America today.

Shabtai Alboher, a Jewish lawyer from New York, who recently made Aliyah asks in a recent *Jerusalem Post* article:

Why are Jewish activists not protesting at the United States Embassy in Tel Aviv demanding, "LET MY PEOPLE GO?" Everyone assumes, of course, that American Jews are free to join their brethren in the Jewish state. But, in reality, American Jews are acting like an oppressed nation that has subordinated its national identity, perhaps unwittingly, to an adopted society and culture.

Despite their physical freedom, American Jews have become enslaved intellectually, emotionally and economically to a materialistic consumer culture that worships dollars and idolizes individual gain and material gratification.

As thousands of Soviet Jews risk economic hardship, torture, and "Siberian vacations" to touch the cherished soil of Israel, American Jews, shackled to their freedom, dial their stockbrokers and plan to exit to kosher Carribbean resorts.

Out of a Jewish community about one-third the size of that in the U.S., approximately 165,000 Jews, have immigrated to Israel from the U.S.S.R. since 1948, compared to only about 60,000 from the "land of the free," America.

Many believe that Israel could not exist without Jewish philanthropic support. American and other Jews use this to justify not making Aliyah, but this is not true. In an article called, "GIVE US PEOPLE, NOT CASH," in the *Jerusalem Post*, dated December 5, 1987, Shlomo Anineri says,

Let us seriously consider emanicipating Israel from direct financial dependence on Jewish philanthropy. The United Jewish Appeal and its affiliates should be abolished.

All worldwide Jewish Fundraising amounts on an annual basis to about 2% of Israel's budget. . . . It is obvious that the Israeli leaders, who mainly address Jewish audiences abroad on fundraising occasions, find it intrinsically difficult to tackle the quest of Aliyah at the same time.

Israel does not need overseas Jewish philanthropy for its survival. No, it needs the Jewish people in the Diaspora to (make Aliyah) come home with whatever money they may have to Israel, their promised land.

Materialism is not the only issue. The Jewish people have been so persecuted for thousands of years, many no longer want to face their Jewishness. They need their faith rebuilt to return to Israel. May God give them strength, faith, courage and hope to resettle one last time before their Messiah comes.

Anatoly Scharansky, a man of great faith, said in Washington, D.C.:

I believe it would be more difficult to live in America than the Soviet Union, because in Russia you know who your enemy is; consequently, you can deal with him; but in the United States, there so many subtle enemies which could disguise themselves as your friends such as materialism (mammon), sensuality, pride, the cares of this world, etc., that it's more difficult to know who and what you are fighting."

There are so many choices to make in America, consequently, things can be more complex and difficult.

It is obviously more difficult to break from the materialistic culture of America than to break from Russia and return to Israel. Looking at percentages, only one American Jew made Aliyah to every eight Soviet Jews over the last 40 years.

We increasingly realize the degree of bondage the Jewish people and Christians in America have to the god of materialism. We print on our money, "In God We Trust," but it seems that the god we trust is the very money on which we are printing, "In God We Trust."

The exposure of the god of mammon seducing a major Christian ministry in American in 1987 is only an extreme case of how many others of us as Christians and Jews have been seduced to lesser degrees. We have to struggle personally to make decisions based on obeying God and doing the things He is calling us to do and to resist the temptation of doing the accepted thing that would appear to be more financially beneficial. I Timothy 6:10 says that the love of money is the root of all kinds of evil, Matthew 6:24 says: "No one can serve two masters because he will love the one and hate the other. You cannot serve God and mammon."

Many in the Jewish and Christian communities have been deceived and seduced by these false gods. We have not taken the Second Commandment seriously which states:

"Thou shalt have no other gods before me."   Exodus 20:3 KJV

We have not discerned the false gods of our contemporary culture: greed, sexual perversion, sensuality, and selfishness which are all manifestations of materialism. Consequently, we have not been able to see the forest for the trees.

The abortionists, drug pushers, pimps and prostitutes, corporate executives, sports heroes, Hollywood and rock star heroes and common laborers who are trying to keep up with the Joneses, nominal and religious Christians and Jews alike, have been bound by materialism of many different forms.

As the Prophet Jonah warned Nineveh of coming judgment, he quoted the following:

Those who cling to worthless idols forfeit the grace that could be theirs.
Jonah 2:8

According to the August 27, 1987, issue of the *Jerusalem Post,* one-thousand Jews a month are leaving the Soviet Union. Only 10% of the more secular Jews leaving are going to Israel while 100% of the Torah-based religious Jews are returning to Israel. The god of materialism in America is so strong, it even blinds and stops the Torah-based orthodox and other religious Jews, including Messianic Jews, in America from following the over 700 scriptures, calling them back to the Land.* May the scriptures and the example of the religious Soviet Jews provoke religious American Jews to follow the Torah in making Aliyah.

Unless the god of mammon in America can be cast out of the church and Jewish people through prayer, God will move to bring down Wall Street and materialism in America;** because He is a jealous God and will have no other gods before Him.

In 1857, within a few weeks after Wall Street fell, the greatest prayer revival in American history began in New York led by Jeremiah Lampheir, and spread across America. Churches were filled throughout New York and America to pray every noon. In some towns, businesses even shut down to pray! God may cause our economy to fall so that people might again cry out to the true God of Israel.

It is time for the Jews to escape the Daughter of Babylon before it's too late. Today is the day of deliverance for the Jewish people. Today you can return to Israel and take your finances with you as Isaiah 60 says the wealth of the nations should be taken back to Israel! If Isaiah 60 is speaking to anyone today, it

*See 700 scriptures in Appendix A.
**This conclusion was drawn in September 1987 before the recent "Black Monday."

is primarily to the Jewish people in America, not the Soviet Union. America is where two-thirds of the Jews in the Disapora live, and where most of the money is!

If the Jewish people don't follow God's call to the land of Israel, when Wall Street and our economy falls completely, the Jews could become a scapegoat, as they have many times in history. They were blamed during the Black Death in Europe; one of the worst plagues in history, and during the Dreyfus case in France (the homeland of liberty and the great revolution) when a Jewish Army Officer was falsely accused of selling military secrets to Germany. They were targeted in the pogroms in Russia in the 1800's before the revolution. Today the Jewish people are falsely accused in Communist countries. In the Middle East, Israel is the scapegoat for many problems that arise there.

When Wall Street and the American economy falls, the Jews could once again be falsely accused. The new director of the Federal Reserve, Alan Greenspan, is Jewish and said he believes there will be a recession by the end of 1988! A fall of Wall Street or depression of our economy could spark increased anti-Semitism throughout America as happened with Fr. McLaughlin during the "Great Depression" of the 1930's.

God wants the Jewish people to go to Israel with their money just as they came out of Egypt to Israel. He wants them to take whatever riches they have in the nations back to Israel before the Stock Market and economy collapses in America. Today is the day of full deliverance. If they wait much longer, because of the coming judgments on America, they will probably go back with nothing, if they are able to return at all!

Lester Sumrall says in his recent book *2000 A.D.* that Jerusalem will be the richest city in the world by the year 2000. If this is true, investing in Jerusalem today could prove to be the best investment in the world.

On November 2, 1987, God gave to the Venezulean pastor, Jaime Puertas, a vision in Jerusalem showing him that the United States of America is preparing a law that will forbid money to be taken out of America in large amounts. The Jews who believe in the prophecy will hurry to sell their possessions, before the law is enacted. They will return bringing the riches of the nations

(Isaiah 60:5), and full of blessings, as the fat cows that Pharoah dreamed (Gen. 41). . . . But he who will not believe has to return with empty sacks, and mourning as the lean, ugly cows because of their unbelief. This law is already in force in Latin America and Spain (Malachi 3:18), and will be adopted by other nations. (Pastor Puertas has started 2,000 congregations in Spanish speaking countries. He had just completed a 40-day fast along with 120 others from his congregations for the "Return of the Captives of Zion to Israel" when he received the vision).

May the American Jews not repeat the tragedy of the history of the Jewish State. Approximately 90% of those who have returned have waited until they were refugees; the poor, lame, halt and blind from the nations.

May Wall Street "Let My People Go!" May God execute His judgments on the god of materialism. May the Jewish people break from materialism in America and escape to Israel before it's too late!

Isaiah 60:5 says the wealth of the seas and the riches of the nations will be brought to Israel. Not only are the Jewish people to take themselves and their money back to Israel, but this verse says others will bring the riches of the nations to Israel as well. May God give the Jewish people favor in America as He did in Egypt so that Americans will give them money to bless Israel.

> Now the Lord had said to Moses, "I will bring one more plague on Pharoah and on Egypt. After that, he will let you go from here, and when he does, he will drive you out completely. Tell the people that men and women alike are to ask their neighbors for articles of silver and gold." Exodus 11:1-2

May God lift the veil from the eyes of Christians and increasingly lead them to help the Jewish people fulfill this scripture by also investing their money in Israel and encouraging others to do the same.

Precious Jewish people, it's time to stop saying "I'm an American Jew," stop bowing down and worshipping the god of materialism in America and fulfill your end-time biblical destiny. Return to the land of your forefathers to worship the God of Abraham, Isaac and Jacob with all your heart!

8 Jewish and Christian Zionism

The Lord had said to Abraham, "Leave your country, your people and your father's household, go to the land I will show you. I will make you into a great nation and I will bless you; I will make your name great, and you will be a blessing. I will bless those who bless you, and whoever curses you I will curse; and all peoples on earth will be blessed through you."
Genesis 12:1-3

The Lord will have compassion on Jacob; once again he will choose Israel and will settle them in their own land. Aliens will join them and unite with the house of Jacob. Nations will take them and bring them to their own place. And the house of Israel will possess the nations as menservants and maidservants in the Lord's land.
Isaiah 14:1, 2

And foreigners who bind themselves to the Lord to serve him, to love the name of the Lord, and to worship him, all who keep the Sabbath without desecrating it and who hold fast to my covenant — these I will bring to my holy mountain and give them joy in my house of prayer. Their burnt offerings and sacrifices will be accepted on my altar; for my house will be called a house of prayer for all nations." The Sovereign Lord declares — he who gathers the exiles of Israel: "I will gather still others to them besides those already gathered."
Isaiah 56:6-8

God has continually been joining Jewish people and Christians together to pray and work for the rebirth and restoration of Israel and the third return of the Jewish people to their promised land for almost 400 years.

Zionism has its roots with Abraham who first immigrated to Jerusalem 4,000 years ago. Abraham was neither a Jew nor a Christian but a man who followed God; going out not knowing where he was going. Abraham was looking for the heavenly Jerusalem who's builder and maker is God when God led him to discover the earthly Jerusalem (Hebrews 11:8-10). He is the Father of all Jewish and Christian Zionists. There have been millions of natural Zionists since that time who have made Aliyah and lived and worked as practical Zionists in the Land of Israel, and millions of others who have helped from afar in the Diaspora. There have also been hundreds of millions of spiritual Zionists, many who have not understood God's purposes for natural Zion.

Biblically, a true Jewish or Christian Zionist believes in both a natural and spiritual Zion as did King David. A Zionist biblically is someone who is seeking and following God with all his heart as Abraham our father did. Anyone who does that will eventually come to understand both natural and spiritual Zion.

Zion within the Bible, in the Old and New Testaments, has several natural meanings. It refers first of all, to physical Zion, Mount Zion, where David brought the Ark of the Covenant in Jerusalem, as well as the City of Jerusalem and even the Land of Israel as a whole (Psalm 48:2; Psalm 137).

Spiritually, Zion in the Old Tesament and New Testament refers to the Presence of God. The writer of the Hebrews says, "We have come to Mount Zion — the city of the living God, the heavenly Jerusalem, and to myriads of angels in joyful assembly" (Hebrews 12:22).

King David believed in the heart of Zion as Jerusalem and Israel, but it wasn't until the Ark with God's Presence came to Zion that the natural and spiritual dimension of Zion became one.

Biblically, there have been many Jewish Zionists, like Joshua and Caleb, who led the first return and Ezra, Nehemiah and Zerubbabel who led the second return.

Ruth is a well-known example of a non-Jewish Zionist from

biblical times, but there also were many others.

The term "modern-day Zionism" appeared first in 1890. Theodore Herzl is the father of modern-day Zionism. He wrote the *Jewish State* and called the first Zionist conference in Basel, Switzerland in 1897. But many Jewish and Christian Zionists worked together as precursors of this return to the Land by preparing the way for Herzl.

The following examples relate how Jewish and Christian Zionists worked together for the restoration of Israel and helped prepare the way for this third return of the Jewish people to the Land.

In 1200 A.D., St. Francis of Assisi, who was going to fight in the Crusades, had a vision. God told him to leave the Crusades, and give away his horse and all his belongings and follow Jesus as a true Christian. He led a pilgrimage to Jerusalem at the beginning of the 13th century and started an Order. The Franciscans were the sole guardians of the Holy Places. The Franciscans, Duns Scotus and William of Occom, were known as forerunners of the Christian Zionists as early as the 13th century.

But the time of Christian Zionism did not really begin until 1609. It was then that Thomas Brightman, a Christian theologian known as the father of the "British Doctrine of Restoration of the Jews," wrote in *THE VISION WAS THERE;* "The Jews will go to Palestine and thus restore their kingdom. There is nothing more certain, the prophets everywhere confirm it."

In 1649 A.D. two English Puritans (Christians) of Amsterdam, Joanna and Ebenezer Cartwright petitioned "That the nation of England with the inhabitants of the Netherlands shall be the first and readiest to transport Israel's sons and daughters on ships to the land of their forefathers, Abraham, Isaac and Jacob, their everlasting possession." This petition to the English government had two parts: 1) England is to assist in restoration of the people of Israel to the land of Palestine; and, 2) Lift the 350-year ban of Jews in England.

Manasseh ben Israel, a learned rabbi of Amsterdam, published a book called *THE HOPE OF ISRAEL* in 1650. What Manasseh had in mind was to open England to the Jews in order that the Diaspora would be truly worldwide. This was necessary before the ingathering of the exiles could begin.

In 1655, Manasseh ben Israel and three other rabbis traveled to London from Amsterdam (invited by Oliver Cromwell) and convinced the English Parliament to compromise and receive the Jewish people into England. Cromwell's interest in Manasseh ben Israel was the stepping-stone to other joinings of Jewish and Christian Zionists to accomplish God's purposes in the restoration of Israel in the years to follow. In 1660, Jews were re-admitted to England.

1840 A.D. — Lord Shaftesbury was said to be the purest man in Westminister. He may have done more for the poor than any man in government throughout history. Charles Dickens called his "10-Hour Bill," the finest piece of legislation ever enacted in England up to that time. Shaftesbury and many with him in the Great Awakening espoused the restoration of Israel as did the Puritans 200 years before him.

In 1840, *THE LONDON TIMES* published Lord Shaftesbury's plan to plant the Jewish people in the land of their forefathers. He was successful in establishing an Anglican Bishopric in Jerusalem and an Anglican Israel on the shores of Palestine, according to *THE BIBLE AND THE SWORD* by Barbara Tuchman.

An Orthodox Jewish friend of Shaftesbury in England, Sir Moses Montefiore believed, like him, in the literal restoration of the Jewish State and worked together with him towards this end. Montefiore and Shaftesbury were another example of Jewish and Christian Zionists who worked together before the rebirth of Israel.

This was still at a time when the Jews themselves had not yet come to believe the idea of a Jewish State. It was another 55 years until Herzl wrote the book, *THE JEWISH STATE.*

1845 — Mordecai Manuel Noah published the *DISCOURSE ON THE RESTORATION OF THE JEWS* in the U.S.A.

It was the first attempt to bring the restoration doctrine into accord with Jewish concepts since Menasseh ben Israel. Noah declared that the United States will pave the way for the restoration to Zion!

He said, "Christian and Jew will, together on Mount Zion, raise their voices in praise of Him whose covenant with Abraham was to endure forever and in whose seed all the nations of the earth are to be blessed." He had no hesitation in advocating a more candid union between Christians and Jews. Noah declared, "Nothing in my opinion will save the nation from sinking into oblivion, but agitating this subject of restoration. We should pass the word around the world, "Restoration of the Jews, 'Justice to Israel,' 'The rights and independence of the Hebrews,' 'Restore them to their country,' 'Redeem them from captivity.' " Christians should be involved to aid them in this good cause.

Mordecai Manuel Noah was a prophetic voice before his time. He was speaking to our generation. Today Jewish and Christian Zionists are cooperating to help in the return of the Jews and are raising their voices together in praise on Mt. Zion.

Herzl, the founder of modern-day Zionism, met William Heckler, a Christian Zionist and chaplain of the British Embassy in Vienna, Austria, in 1896. The providential meeting occurred while Herzl was working as a newspaper reporter on the Dreyfus case. Heckler initially and continually encouraged Herzl and other Zionist leaders for more than 50 years that their movement was of God. They met one month after Herzl completed the book, THE JEWISH STATE. Heckler deduced that 1897 would mark the dawn of the final restoration of Israel in the promised land. Heckler announced this to princes, a statesman and ecclesiastical dignitaries and introduced many of them to Herzl. Herzl started publishing Die Welt a weekly newspaper for the Zionist Movement in 1896 before the First Zionist Conference. In August 1897, 200 delegates met in Basel to hold the First Zionist Congress and founded the World Zionist Organization. Herzl predicted that within five to 50 years a Zionist State would be re-established, which happened exactly 50 years later.

Chaim Weizman, who later became the first president of Israel, lived and worked closely with Lord Balfour, a Christian Zionist in the British Government in London, to bring about the Balfour Declaration in 1917, paving the way for the rebirth of the nation of Israel 30 years later (see Appendix B).

Rees Howells, a Christian Zionist and great intercessor, who headed a Bible school in Wales, had his students praying for the Jews for a long time, but in September 1938 he received a special burden from the Lord. When he heard all the Jews had to leave

Italy within six months and anti-Semitism was rising rapidly in Germany he turned his thoughts toward the return of the Jews to their homeland. He and his students prayed for hours at a time on a regular basis for the rebirth of Israel as a Jewish homeland until it happened 10 years later. May God raise up others in our day to birth an even greater Aliyah movement and outpouring of the Spirit than happened in the first half of this century.

In 1985, 97 years after Herzl held the first Zionist Conference in Basel, Switzerland, the International Christian Embassy in Jerusalem held a Christian Zionist Congress in Basel which was attended by 500 participants from all over the world. In 1988 on the 40th anniversary of Israel's rebirth, the Christian Embassy scheduled the second Christian Zionist Congress in Jerusalem.

The work of the Christian Embassy and many other Christian Zionists has been a great encouragement to Zionism worldwide, and as the nations become increasingly hostile toward Israel, the Christians are saying, "Israel, you are not alone."

Jewish and Christian Zionists alike are commanded in Psalm 122:6 to pray for the peace of Jerusalem that God's shalom may be upon Jerusalem which is the key to world redemption, reconciliation and restoration. Praying for the peace of Jerusalem is a responsibilty for all of God's people throughout the world. May we be faithful to Him in obeying this commandment.

Isaiah 62:6, 7 says, "I have posted watchmen on your walls, O Jerusalem, they will never be silent day or night." You who call on the Lord, give yourselves no rest and give Him no rest until He does two things: 1) Establishes Jerusalem — this happened in 1967 but is continuing through Aliyah from the nations and is the natural restoration of Zion; and, 2) Makes Jerusalem the Praise of all the earth, which is the spiritual restoration of Zion. It is time for all Jews, but especially Torah-based Jewish people who are filled with the Ruach Hakodesh of God, who know how to praise Him, to return to the Land and for the veil over the City of Jerusalem to be lifted and God's Glory to fall on Jerusalem. It is time for the ark of God's Presence to return to Jerusalem in unprecedented ways. This will happen as His redeemed people move into biblical praise and worship and break through the veil. Then His anointing will fall and break every yoke and the strongholds over Jerusalem and the glory of the Lord will cover the earth as the waters cover the seas.

As Jewish and Christian Zionists, may we work together and find our destiny in God by following the example of those who went before us. May we be faithful in praying, warning, helping and participating in what may well be the last and hopefully the greatest wave of Aliyah in this century before severe judgments fall on America and other gentile nations.

Isaiah 2:3 says the law will go forth from Zion and the word of the Lord from Jerusalem in the last days. May God give us the courage as Jewish and Christian Zionists to blow the trumpet in unison from Zion and sound the alarm together in America. Jewish people, come home to Jerusalem to worship and praise the High God of heaven with all your heart so He can make Jerusalem a "praise" in all the earth!

9 Christians: A Time to Pray A Time to Warn, And a Time to Help

> Comfort, comfort my people, says your God. Speak tenderly to Jerusalem, and proclaim to her that her hard service has been completed, that her sin has been paid for, that she has received from the Lord's hand double for all her sins. A voice of one calling: "In the desert prepare the way for the Lord; make straight in the wilderness a highway for our God." Every valley shall be raised up, every mountain and hill made low; the rough ground shall become level, the rugged places a plain. And the glory of the Lord will be revealed, and all mankind together will see it. For the mouth of the Lord has spoken.
>
> Isaiah 40:1-5

> This is what the sovereign Lord says: "See, I will beckon to the Gentiles, I will lift up my banner to the peoples; they will bring your sons in their arms and carry your daughters on their shoulders."
>
> Isaiah 49:22

Christians have a tremendous debt to the Jewish people. They have given us the prophets and apostles, our Bible, our heritage in the land of Israel and our Messiah. Now is the time to show our appreciation by praying, warning and helping the Jewish people in America.

In the Old Testament (Tenach), God says through the prophet Malachi that He will turn the hearts of the fathers to their children and the hearts of the children to their fathers before the great and dreadful Day of the Lord comes.

Despite the great division, persecution and tragedy throughout history, truly in our day, God is turning the hearts of the Jews towards the Christians and the hearts of the true Christians to the Jews throughout the world. Amazing things have happened just within the decade of the 80's between Evangelical Christians and Jews. At the same time the nations of the world are turning against Israel.

We live in days where it appears Zechariah 14:2 may soon be fulfilled, "I will gather all nations to Jerusalem to fight against it." The Lord will go out and fight against those nations as He fought in the day of battle. His feet will stand on the Mount of Olives. The Messiah of the Bible, for whom the Jews and Christians are looking, could come very soon. Some orthodox Jews are now wearing buttons stating, "We want Mashiach now!" Christians are also expecting His soon appearing.

All nations, probably including the U.S., will withdraw support from Israel as mentioned in Zechariah 14:2, and the only allies the Jews and Israel may have in the world will be the true Christians. Some people believe that God is restoring Ephraim (Christians) and Judah (Jews) of Ezekiel 37:19-20 into one stick and that the Jews and Christians may be the two witnesses in Revelation.

Before long, the Jews will increasingly realize that the only true friends they have in the world are true Christians and vice versa! The Jewish People, in spite of the terrible things nominal Christians have done to them over the centuries, are also accepting the Christians. Prime Ministers of Israel and the Mayor of Jerusalem have been very gracious and kind to Christians.

Jewish lay people and rabbis, by God's grace, are rising above the terrible sins of nominal Christians of the past and loving and being loved by Christians today. God is putting His love in the hearts of the Jewish fathers towards their Christian children and vice versa. Christians are being welcomed in synagogues at Passover seders, at Israeli embassies and all kinds of special gatherings to support Israel and the Jewish people.

At the turn of the decade, Christians representing many

nations opened a Christian Embassy in Jerusalem at the same time the nations were moving their embassies out of Jerusalem to Tel Aviv because of political pressure. An annual Christian Celebration of the Feast of Tabernacles also began at that time which now is drawing approximately 5,000 Christians to Jerusalem each fall. During this week-long celebration it is truly exciting to see thousands of Christians participate in the Great Jerusalem march with the Jewish people.

In addition, national celebrations for the rebirth of Israel, National Israel Prayer Breakfasts, Israel days, local Christian celebrations of the Feasts of Tabernacles, and many dialogue meetings between Christians and Jews have been happening over the last seven years in America and in many other nations.

God seems to be birthing a supernatural love in the hearts of the Christians for the Jewish people. Isaiah 40 is being fulfilled which says:

Comfort, comfort my people. Speak tenderly to Jerusalem, prepare the way for the Lord, make straight in the wilderness, a highway for our God.

This sovereign moving of God's Spirit between Christians and Jews has been expressed by much love and many gifts given to Israel and Jews of other nations by Christians. The timing of this supernatural move of God, in restoring the hearts of Christians to the Jewish people and the Jewish people to the Christians, is in God's divine providence!

Just as God used the Jews in the first century to take the message of the Lord to the world, so He is beginning to use the Christians in this hour to comfort and warn and help the Jews to return to Israel before judgment comes on the Gentile nations.

We have seen this already happening in regards to Soviet Jewry with thousands of Christians praying for the release of the Jews from the Soviet Union, although only a small number have been able to actually go behind the Iron Curtain to Russia and help.

Can you imagine the impact of not only rabbis and other Jewish prophetic voices encouraging the Jews to return to Israel, but also in America and all over the world; thousands of Spirit-filled Christians praying, warning and helping the Jews to return to their beloved Israel before it's too late?

First, we need to pray and fast that God will break the veil of the god of materialism from all eyes — Jewish and Gentile. We must deal with our own hearts and lives so we can approach our Jewish brethren with purity of heart and a humble spirit. Only then can we act in true love. We have started a fast to break the power of materialism. We will continue this fast (with different people each taking a week or more to fast) until the Jewish people return from America to Israel their everlasting possession and homeland.

Areas of Prayers on Which to Focus:

1. Pray for the Jewish people to return to God and to love Him with all their heart, soul, mind and strength.

2. Pray for all branches of Judaism to take seriously the 700 scriptures about the Jewish people returning to Israel (they are listed in the back of the book), and to pray, meditate on and obey them. Pray that the word of God in those scriptures will break the power of our materialistic and communistic cultures which would stop them from following God's call home.

3. Many scriptures have been applied spiritually for centuries, it is now time to pray for their literal fulfillment. Just as Larry Lea and others have applied Isaiah 43:4-5 spiritually, we need to bind the forces that are holding the Jewish people and pray for the literal fulfillment of the Jewish people coming home.

4. Pray for thousands of intercessors to be raised up in America to pray that the god of materialism and the cares of this life that have the Jews and Christians in America in bondage be cast off. May they prophesy and say: "Let my people go!" to the god of materialism.

5. Pray for God to raise up thousands of Jewish and Christian Zionist voices throughout America to warn and help the Jewish people escape from America to Israel.

6. Pray that the Jewish and Christian community will do everything possible to encourage Aliyah (immigration to Israel) and help practically. May we make this a biblical priority.

7. Pray that Jewish people will return as soon as possible and take their finances with them to bless Israel, their future generations, and to prepare the land for the return of the Soviet Jews. May this happen before Wall Street falls completely and our economy falls to such an extent that they go back with nothing as refugees.

8. Pray that the Jewish people of America will have tender hearts to God's call and respond to the warnings before increasing judgments fall on America and they have to deal with those who would try to destroy them.

9. Pray that the American Jews become an example and become practical Zionists by returning to Israel, preparing the way and welcoming the Soviet Jews to Israel, thus discouraging them from coming to America to be seduced by the god of materialism.

10. Pray for thousands of Christian Zionists in America, that they may take up their prophetic mantle and *lay down their lives* for the Jewish people in America and help them in any way possible to return to Israel. This is our opportunity to show our love and gratefulness to the Jewish people for all they have done for us throughout history. Also, you could take this book and give it to your Jewish friends and offer to help your Jewish neighbors to prepare to move there by buying a plane ticket or helping with a down payment to rent or buy a house or an apartment in Israel. We need to warn and help the Jews to return before it's too late! One large church is believing God for one million dollars to help the Jewish people return to Israel. Your church, or you as an individual, could be a great blessing to His chosen people. The Holy Spirit will show you many other creative ways you can pray for, warn, love and help them. Unless the Jews respond quickly and return to Israel, many may not be able to

return at all.

Once, while driving in New York, I had a vision of a network of "cities of refuge" all over America where suffering Jews would be cared for by Christians. I have since found out that many Christians are already preparing houses of refuge in rural areas throughout America for the Jews who fail to escape to Israel. These places are for those who survive AIDS, financial collapse, anti-Semitic attacks, terrorist attacks and possible nuclear attacks.

I also recently met a woman who claims to have had a vision that 14,000 Soviet Jews were going to come out through Alaska and that Christians were preparing to care for them in cities of refuge in America, hoping to help them return to Israel.

While the cities of refuge are important for those few who survive the judgments in America, God's mandate to me is to warn the Jews to return to Israel immediately in order to ensure their survival. In fact, Ezekiel 39:20 says that none will be left in the Diaspora, implying that they will either be killed or return to Israel. Consequently, most of the time and money invested should help and encourage the Jewish people to return to Israel and help them settle in their land, avoiding years in the wilderness on the way.

I'm learning that loving the Jewish people goes beyond praying for them, holding banquets and prayer breakfasts, taking tours to Israel, planting trees in Israel and taking clothes to Russia or Israel. As good as those things are, true love is tough love and is warning the Jewish people to return to Israel and offering to help them even when they think you're crazy or reject you. Don't forget that historically prophetic warnings were initially rejected. If only there would have been more righteous Gentiles in Europe in the 1930's to warn and help the Jews escape!

"Blessed are they which are persecuted for righteousness' sake, for theirs is the kingdom of heaven."   Matthew 5:10 KJV

Those of you whom God is speaking this to as a prophetic word have a responsibility to warn the Jewish people as Ezekiel 3:16-19 states: If we warn them, then we will not be held accountable, but if we do not, their blood will be on our hands.

The hour is later than we think! Many intercessors and prophets are having visions and dreams of bombs going off and devastations coming to America.

> Blow the trumpet in Zion; sound the alarm on my holy mountain. Let all who live in the land tremble, for the day of the Lord is coming. It is close at hand.   Joel 2:1

Pray for the Jewish people. Break the god of mammon off of their backs in prayer. Take up your prophetic mantle. Blow a trumpet in Zion! Sound an alarm on My holy mountain to our precious Jewish people in America! Encourage them immediately to escape the Daughter of Babylon and return to Israel before it is too late! Many of you may also be called to help them return.

Isaiah 49:22 refers to the role Gentiles have to play in helping the Jews return: We shall bring the sons in our arms and the daughters shall be carried on our shoulders, back to Israel.

I believe God is calling some righteous Gentiles not only to warn and help the Jews return, but He may also give some of them an inheritance in the land of Israel with the Jewish people. Some of us like Ruth of old, will say, "Where you go, I will go, and where you lodge, I will lodge. Your people shall be my people. Your God shall be my God!" God will bless those who bless His people!

Israel needs many righteous Gentiles (true Christians) to warn, love and assist the Jewish people at this time. Discern the times in which you live and know what you should do. There is a time for everything under heaven. It is truly a time to pray, a time to warn and a time to help the Jewish people to return to Israel. It is a time to fulfill your end-time destiny as a lover of Zion!

10 "Deliver Thyself O Zion" Escape from the Daughter of Babylon

Win the Struggle, Come Home to Israel

"Deliver thyself, O Zion, escape from the Daughter of Babylon."
Zechariah 2:7 KJV

"For our struggle is not against flesh and blood but against the rulers, against the authorities, against the powers of this dark world and against the spiritual forces of evil in the heavenly realm."
Ephesians 6:12

Set up road signs; put up guideposts. Take note of the highway, the road that you take. Return, O Virgin Israel, return to your towns. How long will you wander, O unfaithful daughter?
Jeremiah 31:21

"However, the days are coming," declares the Lord, "when men will no longer say, 'As surely as the Lord lives, who brought the Israelites up out of Egypt,' but will say, 'As surely as the Lord lives, who brought the Israelites up out of the land of the north and out of all the countries (including America!) where he had banished them.' For I will restore them to the land I gave their forefathers. But now I will send for many fishers," declares the Lord, "and they will catch them. After that I will send for many hunters, and they will hunt them down on every mountain and hill and from the crevices of the rocks."
Jeremiah 16:14-16

And everyone who calls on the name of the Lord will be saved; for on Mount Zion and in Jerusalem there will be deliverance, as the Lord has said, among the survivors whom the Lord calls.   Joel 2:32

Every one of the 88 civilizations of man's history has eventually fallen; many through corruption from within and others by an attack from without. The United States of America is one of the first major civilizations to last over 200 years (1776-1987) as a leading world power.

America has served as a great blessing to the Jewish people

and to the world, however, its internal decay is beginning to eat away her strength. The decay of America has been increasing gradually over the last generation. As sin and decadence continue to accelerate, it is only God's mercy that we have lasted this long as a world power.

Lester Sumrall said in his book *JERUSALEM: WHERE EMPIRES DIE,* 1984:

> What has become of the United States since 1956? Note carefully. We have lost the last two wars we have fought, in Korea and Vietnam. Our society has begun to fall apart rapidly. Violent rebellion broke out on our college campuses. The drug problem, sexual sin, and divorce have exploded. Our economy has become far less stable and far more vulnerable to foreign competition.
>
> All these things may seem unrelated on the surface, but that is not the case. It is not a coincidence that these problems erupted after our desertion of Israel in 1956. And this turning away, however gradual has continued in recent years as we have sought to please oil sheiks. Thus, like Babylon, Persia, Rome, and all the others, America has put its hand into the golden bowl of Jerusalem and is in imminent danger of being put on the shelf by God, so to speak, as a world power.

Will the U.S. repeat the mistakes of England and stop supporting Israel after blessing her for hundreds of years? May God give America the grace to continue supporting Israel as she becomes the head and not the tail and a banner for the nations. Sumrall continues:

> If there is no revival and renewed commitment to Israel, I can see the moral degradation of our day growing ever more widespread and severe, and the United States decaying from within, as did Rome and many other great empires of the past. Perhaps then Russia could force us to our knees.

Also since 1956 prayer and Bible reading were removed from our schools and abortion was legalized in America.

Unfortunately, not only is the secular American and international society today turning against Israel, but so is much of the nominal church. It was not until 1982 that God lifted the veil from my eyes to see His purposes for Israel in these last days.

Because of my blindness in the past I can empathize with many Christians who adhere to replacement theology today. We need to love them, pray for God to lift the veil from their eyes, and help them see the truth in regards to God's purposes for Israel and the Jewish people today.

The story of church history has been that many times the leaders of the last move of God rejected and persecuted the people who were in the forefront of God's ongoing purposes. The Catholics persecuted Luther; Luther and Calvin persecuted and condoned the killings of the Anabaptists; many of the traditional churches rejected the Jesus movement; the Assemblies of God initially rejected the Charismatic movement. Unless the veil is removed from Christians who believe in replacement theology they could reject the coming outpouring of the Holy Spirit on Israel and even persecute the Jewish people. If Catholic and Lutheran theology in many ways paved the way for the Inquisition and Holocaust, I hate to think what kind of persecution could come in the near future toward the Jewish people unless God lifts the veil from the eyes of the nominal Christians.

> This is the word of the Lord concerning Israel. The Lord, who stretches out the heavens, who lays the foundation of the earth, and who forms the spirit of man within him, declares. "I am going to make Jerusalem a cup that sends all the surrounding peoples reeling. Judah will be besieged as well as Jerusalem. On that day, when all the nations of the earth are gathered against her, I will make Jerusalem an immovable rock for all the nations. All who try to move it will injure (rupture) themselves. On that day I will strike every horse with panic and its rider with madness," declares the Lord. "I will keep a watchful eye over the house of Judah, but I will blind all the horses of the nations."
> Zechariah 12:1-4

Israel will be the next and last major civilization of man according to the Bible. The land of Israel was given to the Jews as an everlasting and eternal possession as promised in Genesis 17:8. The Jewish Patriarchs realized this, to the point they even had their bones buried there if they died outside Israel. It is again time to favor Zion. It is time to take the spiritual Ark back to Jerusalem. God will soon pour out greater judgments on America and other Gentile nations and a greater spiritual awakening will come on Israel.

People ask: Why did God allow the Holocaust in Europe?

For years, a loving God warned the Jews to leave through the Jewish Zionist prophets, but 90% of them refused to leave before it was too late! If more than 10% of the Jews leave America before it falls or becomes a lesser power, it would be one of the first times in history. Zechariah 12:8 says that two-thirds of the Jews in the world would be killed. One-third of them, six million, have already been killed in the Holocaust. I am concerned that six million more could be devastated in America unless they return soon. God says in Jeremiah 16:16 that He will send for many fishers to warn and help them to return to Israel. In Europe, the fishers were the Zionists and the hunters were the Nazis. Today in America, the fishers are the Jewish prophets as well as some Christian Zionists. May the Jewish people respond to the fishers today, or the hunters may soon come. In America they could be the KKK, Islamic terrorists, the KGB, or others.

This book is written with a deep love to warn the Jewish people to escape the Daughter of Babylon (the U.S.A.) because it is about to be greatly devastated. Precious Jewish people, if you don't leave immediately, you may go back with no money, you may be killed or not be able to go back at all!

Repeating what Santayana said: "He who does not learn from the lessons of history is doomed to repeat them." May the Jewish people and America as a nation learn from the recent lessons of history, may the Jewish people return to Israel very soon, and escape impending judgments and another possible Holocaust in America.

Benefits of Making Aliyah Soon!

1. Honor the God of Israel and receive His blessing by obeying His call to return to the land of Israel.

2. Prepare for your children and succeeding generations to live in the land of promise. Many believe Israel will be the next and last major civilization of man before Messiah comes.

3. Escape the coming judgments and difficulties in the falling civilization of the U.S.A.

4. If you return to Israel soon you can take any finances with

you before our economy falls. You can benefit and be a blessing by helping your family, but also the nation by helping take the wealth of the nations back to Israel. Prepare now to prosper in the land of your forefathers!

5. You can help restore the land to blossom as a rose in preparation for the return of millions of Jews from Russia and America in the coming years and welcome them home at the gates of Jerusalem.

6. Experience the blessings of living in the cultural and religious environment of your people and not being assimilated into Gentile cultures.

7. You can participate in the great Jewish Revival coming in the land of Israel as mentioned in Ezekiel 37 and welcome the Messiah.

Things to Do Immediately in Preparation for Making Aliyah Soon!

Every Jewish person in the United States (and the rest of the free world) should wisely and carefully do the following:

1. *Understand the Law of Return:* The State of Israel has a Law of Return which allows all Jews to "return" to Israel and become citizens. (American Jews do not forfeit their U.S. citizenship when they do this.) Normally non-Jewish people have not been able to immigrate to Israel, but a few have received permanent residency for special and unusual service. Also you can stay for an extended period of time on a visitor's passport or a work visa. Make your plans carefully and consult with knowledgeable people from your Congregation or Synagogue about Aliyah.

2. *Change Your Mindset:* Remember that God Almighty has planned and declared that Jews are to be regathered and never again leave Israel:

"And I will bring again the captivity of my people of Israel, and they shall build the waste cities, and inhabit them; and they shall plant vineyards, and drink the wine thereof; they shall also make gardens, and eat the fruit of them. And I will plant them upon their land, and they shall no more be pulled up out of their land which I have given them," saith the Lord thy God. Amos 9:14, 15 KJV

Living in the Land of Israel is equal to all the other commandments in the Torah, Sifrey Re'eh 12:29 Mishnah.

3. Pay off all accounts including credit cards.

4. Go to your local post office and *obtain a passport.*

5. Visit Israel. See what the employment situation is for each profession/vocation, and also the housing. Send for brochures if travel is beyond your budget. Seek out a few "pen pals" to answer your questions.

6. *Hebrew:* Start learning Hebrew while you are still in the Galut. Every bit helps. If possible, take a course that gives you an overview of the linguistic structure and grammar, because Israel's ulpanim (Hebrew-language training programs) never do that. Since most Americans, deep in their hearts, believe that English is the only "real" language in the world, learning Hebrew is their greatest single barrier to getting adjusted in Israel.

7. *Marriage, Children:* If you are single or married, childless or with a family, now is the time to immigrate. Every situation has its advantages so don't wait for a change — go as you are!

8. *Work:* Come with a profession if you can. But before investing years in training, check to see if your skills will be needed, how well such work pays, whether you will be able to work without broad knowledge of Hebrew, and whether it might be better to gain your particular job skills in Israel rather than in the Galut.

9. Solidify the value of your property in America and sell.

10. *Money:* Bring as much of your money and wealth of the nations back to bless Israel as possible as Isaiah 60 says. You should immediately invest as much money in Israel as possible while it can still be taken out of America. (See vision on page 48.)

11. *Housing:* Save as much money as possible to buy property in Israel and buy as soon as possible!

12. *Pray for the Peace of Jerusalem (Psalm 122:6):* For reconciliation and peace with God between Jews and Arabs.

13. Acquire more information from a local Aliyah office in the U.S.A. if necessary.

14. *Go to Israel:* Go directly to Israel, do not "pass" going until the Stock Market climbs or falls or until your son finishes college.

Israel Come Home

> Afterwards the Israelites will return and seek the Lord their God and David their King. They will come trembling to the Lord and to His blessing in the *last days.*   Hosea 3:5

Be a pioneer and follow the Cloud of Glory like your Patriarchs; Abraham, Moses, Joshua, David and others. Fulfill your end-time destiny as a son or daughter of Abraham and live as a practical Zionist in Israel, the land of your forefathers.

The Jews prospered greatly in historic Babylon as they have in America. God gave them a promise that Jeremiah spoke to the Jewish people in Babylon after the 70 years of captivity, if they were obedient to follow the Lord back to the land of Israel.

> "For I know the plans I have for you," declares the Lord, "plans to prosper you and not harm you, plans to give you a hope and a future."   Jeremiah 29:11

I believe this is also applicable to the Jewish people who escape the Babylon of America to Israel today. In Ezekiel 37:13, 14, God says He will bring the Jewish people back to the land of Israel:

> "Then you, my people will know that I am the Lord, I will put my spirit in you and you will live, and I will settle you in your land. . . . Then you will know that I the Lord have spoken and I have done it," says the Lord!

Even though leaving America will mean some initial sacrifices and cultural changes, God promises a great spiritual revival in the land of Israel in the last days that will be much more meaningful and fulfilling than experiencing the economic, moral, military and spiritual disintegration . . . and possibly the soon destruction of America! Beloved Jewish people, the apple of God's eye, don't miss your destiny in Zion! God of materialism, "LET MY PEOPLE GO!"

This third Exodus from the nations and return to Israel will be the greatest and will bring what the first two only began preparing the way for. The third return will usher in the coming of Messiah in all His Glory, everlasting peace to Jerusalem, world redemption and the healing of the nations. It is no wonder Isaiah 51:11 says:

> Therefore, the redeemed of the Lord shall return, and come with singing unto Zion, and everlasting joy shall be upon their head; they shall obtain gladness and joy, and sorrow and mourning shall flee away.
>
> KJV

God says in Zechariah 2:7:

> "Deliver thyself O Zion! Escape you who live in the Daughter of Babylon." KJV

Precious Jewish people, make Aliyah very soon, don't wait until you have to go. Win the struggle and escape to Israel today. Come singing and dancing with joy and gladness to Zion preparing the way for the soon coming of your Messiah and King!

You have not finished reading this book until you have read the 700 Scripture verses in Appendix A!

Appendix A

Scriptural References

To read, pray and meditate on!

Here are over 700 verses of scripture where God promises the Land of Canaan to His chosen people and commands or encourages them to return to the Land of Israel which He gave to them as an everlasting inheritance:

Genesis 12:1-3   (God's promise to Abraham and his descendants) The Lord had said to Abram, "Leave your country, your people and your father's household and go to the land I will show you. I will make you into a great nation and I will bless you; I will make your name great, and you will be a blessing. I will bless those who bless you, and whoever curses you I will curse; and all peoples on earth will be blessed through you."

Genesis 12:6, 7   Abram traveled through the land as far as the site of the great tree of Moreh at Shechem. The Canaanites were then in the land, but the Lord appeared to Abram and said, "To your offspring I will give this land."

Genesis 13:1, 2   Abram went up from Egypt to the Negev, with his wife and everything he had, and Lot went with him. Abram had become very wealthy in livestock and in silver and gold.

Genesis 13:15   There above it stood the Lord, and he said: I am the Lord, the God of your father Abraham and the God of Isaac. I will give you and your descendants the land on which you are lying. Your descendants will be like the dust of the earth, and you will spread out to the west and to the east, to the north and to the south. All peoples on earth will be blessed through you and your offspring. I am with you and will watch over you wherever you go, and I will bring you back to this land. I will not leave you until I have done what I have promised you."

Genesis 13:14-17   The Lord said to Abram after Lot had parted from him, "Lift up your eyes from where you are and look north and south, east and west. All the land that you see I will give to you and your offspring forever. I will make your offspring like the dust of the earth, so that if anyone could count the dust, then your offspring could be counted. Go, walk through the length and breadth of the land, for I am giving it to you."

Genesis 15:7   He (God) also said to him, "I am the Lord, who brought you out of Ur of the Chaldeans to give you this land to take possession of it."

Genesis 15:13-14   Then the Lord said to him, "Know for certain that your descendants will be strangers in a country not their own, and they will be enslaved and mistreated four hundred years. But I will punish the nation they serve as slaves, and afterward they will come out with great possessions.

Genesis 15:18-21   On that day the Lord made a covenant with Abram and said, "To your descendants I give this land, from the river of Egypt to the great river, the Euphrates — the land of the Kenites, Kenizzites, Kadmonites, Hittites, Perizzites, Rephaites, Amorites, Canaanites, Girgashites and Jebusites."

Genesis 17:5-8   "No longer will you be called Abram, your name will be Abraham, for I have made you a father of many nations. I will make you very fruitful; I will make nations of you, and kings will come from you. I will establish my covenant as an everlasting covenant between me and you and your descendants after you for the generations to come, to be your God and the God of your descendants after you. The whole land of Canaan, where you are now an alien, I will give as an everlasting possession to you and your descendants after you; and I will be their God."

Genesis 17:7, 8   "I will establish my covenant as an everlasting covenant between me and you and your descendants after you for the generations to come, to be your God and the God of your descendants after you. The whole land of Canaan, where you are now an alien, I will give as an everlasting possession to you and your descendants after you. And I will be their God."

Genesis 17:19   Then God said, "Yes, but your wife Sarah will bear you a son and you will call him Isaac. I will establish my covenant with him as an everlasting covenant for his descendants after him."

Genesis 18:18-19   "Abraham will surely become a great and powerful nation, and all nations on earth will be blessed through him. For I have chosen him, so that he will direct his children and his household after him to keep the way of the Lord by doing what is right and just, so that the Lord will bring about for Abraham what he has promised him."

Genesis 22:17, 18   "I will surely bless you and make your descendants as numerous as the stars in the sky and as the sand on the seashore. Your descendants will take possession of the cities of their enemies, and through your offspring all nations on earth will be blessed, because you have obeyed me."

Genesis 23:17   (Purchase of Cave of Machpelah — burial site of Patriarchs)

Genesis 25:7-11   (Burial of Abraham in Cave of Machpelah — Hebron)

Genesis 26:3, 4   "Stay in this land for a while, and I will be with you and will bless you. For to you and your descendants I will give all these lands and will confirm the oath I swore to your father Abraham. I will make your descendants as numerous as the stars in the sky and will give them all these lands, and through your offspring all nations on earth will be blessed."

Genesis 26:12   Isaac planted crops in that land and the same year reaped a hundredfold, because the Lord blessed him.

Genesis 26:24   That night the Lord appeared to him and said, "I am the God of your father Abraham. Do not be afraid, for I am with you; I will bless you and increase the number of your descendants for the sake of my servant Abraham."

Genesis 28:3-4   "May God Almighty bless you and make you fruitful and increase your numbers until you become a community of peoples. May he give you and your descendants the blessing of Abraham, so that you may take possession of the land where you now live as an alien, the land God gave to Abraham."

Genesis 28:13-15   There above it stood the Lord, and he said: "I am the Lord, the God of your father Abraham and the God of Isaac. I will give you and your descendants the land on which you are lying. Your descendants will be like the dust of the earth, and you will spread out to the west and to the east, to the north and to the south. All peoples on earth will be blessed through you and your offspring. I am with you and will watch over you wherever you go, and I will bring you back to this land. I will not leave you until I have done what I have promised you."

Genesis 31:3   Then the Lord said to Jacob, "Go back to the land of your fathers and to your relatives, and I will be with you."

Genesis 31:13   "I am the God of Bethel, where you anointed a pillar and where you made a vow to me. Now leave this land at once and go back to your native land."

Genesis 31:17   Then Jacob put his children and his wives on camels and he drove all his livestock ahead of him, along with all the goods he had accumulated in Paddan Aram, to go to his father Isaac in the land of Canaan.

Genesis 32:9, 10   Then Jacob prayed, "O God of my father Abraham, God of my father Isaac, O Lord, who said to me, 'Go back to your country and your relatives, and I will make you prosper,' I am unworthy of all the kindness and faithfulness you have shown your servant.

Genesis 35:10-13   God said to him, "Your name is Jacob, but you will no longer be called Jacob; your name will be Israel." So he named him Israel. And God said to him, "I am God Almighty; be fruitful and increase in number. A nation and a community of nations will come from you, and kings will come from your body. The land I gave to Abraham and Isaac I will give to you, and I will give this land to your descendants after you."

Genesis 35:27-29   (Isaac buried by Esau and Jacob in the promised land)

Genesis 46:3, 4   "I am God, the God of your father," he said, "Do not be afraid to go down to Egypt, for I will make you into a great nation there. I will bring you back again. And Joseph's own hand will close your eyes."

Genesis 48:21   Then Israel (Jacob) said to Joseph, "I am about to die, but God will be with you and take you back to the land of your fathers."

Genesis 49:29-32   (Death of Jacob — Israel — and burial in the promised land) Then he gave them these instructions: "I am about to be gathered to my people. Bury me with my fathers in the cave in the field of Ephron the Hittite, the cave in the field of Machpelah, near Mamre in Canaan, which Abraham bought as a burial place from Ephron the Hittite, along with the field. There Abraham and his wife

Sarah were buried, there Isaac and his wife Rebekah were buried, and there I buried Leah. The field and the cave in it were bought from the Hittites."

Genesis 50:12-15 (Burial in Canaan) So Jacob's sons did as he had commanded them: They carried him to the land of Canaan and buried him in the cave in the field of Machpelah, near Mamre, which Abraham had bought as a burial place from Ephron the Hittite, along with the field. After burying his father, Joseph returned to Egypt, together with his brothers and all the others who had gone with him to bury his father.

Genesis 50:24-25 Then Joseph said to his brothers, "I am about to die. But God will surely come to your aid and take you up out of this land to the land he promised on oath to Abraham, Isaac and Jacob." And Joseph made the sons of Israel swear an oath and said. "God will surely come to your aid, and then you must carry my bones up from this place."

Exodus 1:1-5 (70 descendants of Jacob go down to Egypt to escape famine. About 430 years later (Ex. 12:37, 38) 3,000,000 Jewish people are brought out of Egypt to return to the land God promised them.)

Exodus 2:24 God heard their groaning and He remembered His covenant with Abraham, with Isaac and with Jacob.

Exodus 3:7-8 The Lord said, "I have indeed seen the misery of my people in Egypt. I have heard them crying out because of their slave drivers, and have come down to rescue them from the hand of the Egyptians and to bring them up out of that land into a good and spacious land, a land flowing with milk and honey."

Exodus 6:8 And I will bring you to the land I swore with uplifted hand to give to Abraham, to Isaac and to Jacob. I will give it to you as a possession. I am the Lord.

Exodus 12:24 (THE PASSOVER) "Obey these instructions as a lasting ordinance for you and your descendants. When you enter the land that the Lord will give you as he promised, observe this ceremony."

Exodus 12:35-36 (Taking the wealth out of Egypt) The Israelites did as Moses instructed and asked the Egyptians for articles of silver and gold and for clothing. The Lord had made the Egyptians favorably disposed toward the people, and they gave them what they asked for; so they plundered the Egyptians.

Exodus 13:15   "When the Lord brings you into the land of the Canaanites, Hittites, Amorites, Hivites and Jebusites — the land he swore to your forefathers to give you, a land flowing with milk and honey — you are to observe this ceremony in this month."

Exodus 13:11,12   "After the Lord brings you into the land of the Canaanites and gives it to you, as he promised on oath to you and your forefathers, you are to give over to the Lord the first offspring of every womb. All the first born males of your livestock belong to the Lord."

Exodus 19:5   'Now if you obey me fully and keep my covenant, then out of all nations you will be my treasured possession.'

Exodus 20:2   I am the Lord your God, who brought you out of Egypt, out of the land of slavery.

Exodus 23:20-23   "See, I am sending an angel ahead of you to guard you along the way and to bring you to the place I have prepared. Pay attention to him and listen to what he says. Do not rebel against him; he will not forgive your rebellion, since my Name is in him. If you listen carefully to what he says and do all that I say, I will be an enemy to your enemies and will oppose those who oppose you. My angel will go ahead of you and bring you into the land of the Amorites, Hittites, Perizzites, Cannanites, Hivites and Jebusites, and I will wipe them out."

Exodus 23:31   "I will establish your borders from the Red Sea to the Sea of the Philistines, and from the desert to the River. I will hand over to you the people who live in the land and you will drive them out before you."

Exodus 29:45-46   "Then I will dwell among the Israelites and be their God. They will know that I am the Lord their God, who brought them out of Egypt so that I might dwell among them. I am the Lord their God."

Exodus 32:13   'Remember your servants Abraham, Isaac and Israel, to whom you swore by your own self: "I will make your descendants as numerous as the stars in the sky and I will give your descendants all this land I promised them, and it will be their inheritance forever." '

Exodus 33:1   Then the Lord said to Moses, "Leave this place, you and the people you brought up out of Egypt, and go up to the land I promised on oath to Abraham, Isaac and Jacob, saying 'I will give it to your descendants.' "

Exodus 34:24   "I will drive out nations before you and enlarge your territory, and no one will covet your land when you go up three times each year to appear before the Lord your God."

Leviticus 20:24   "But I said to you, 'You will possess their land; I will give it to you as an inheritance, a land flowing with milk and honey.' I am the Lord your God, who has set you apart from the nations."

Leviticus 25:1,2   The Lord said to Moses on Mt. Sinai, "Speak to the Israelites and say to them: 'When you enter the land I am going to give you, the land itself must observe a sabbath to the Lord.'"

Leviticus 25:10,13   (Year of Jubilee) Consecrate the fiftieth year and proclaim liberty throughout the land to all its inhabitants. It shall be a jubilee for you; each one of you is to return to his family property and each to his own clan. . . . In this Year of Jubilee everyone is to return to his own property.

Leviticus 25:18,19   "Follow my decrees and be careful to obey my laws, and you will live safely in the land. Then the land will yield its fruit, and you will eat your fill and live there in safety."

Leviticus 25:38   I am the Lord your God, who brought you out of Egypt to give you the land of Canaan and to be your God.

Leviticus 25:41   Then he and his children are to be released, and he will go back to his own clan and to the property of his forefathers.

Leviticus 26:9   I will look on you with favor and make you fruitful and increase your numbers, and I will keep my covenant with you.

Leviticus 26:42   I will remember my covenant with Jacob and my covenant with Isaac and my covenant with Abraham, and I will remember the land.

Numbers 10:29   Now Moses said to Hobab, son of Reuel the Midianite, Moses' father-in-law, "We are setting out for the place about which the Lord said, 'I will give it to you.' Come with us and we will treat you well, for the Lord has promised good things to Israel."

Numbers 11:12   "Did I conceive all these people? Did I give them birth? Why do you tell me to carry them in my arms, as a nurse carries an infant, to the land you promised on oath to their forefathers?" (Moses speaking to God)

Numbers 13:1,2   The Lord said to Moses, "Send some men to explore the land of Canaan, which I am giving to the Israelites. From each ancestral tribe send one of its leaders."

Numbers 13:17-20   When Moses sent them to explore Canaan, he said, "Go up through the Negev and on into the hill country. See what the land is like and whether the people who live there are strong or weak, few or many. What kind of land do they live in? Is it good or bad? What kind of towns do they live in? Are they unwalled or fortified? How is the soil? Is it fertile or poor? Are there trees on it or not? Do your best to bring back some of the fruit of the land."

Numbers 14:8   If the Lord is pleased with us, he will lead us into that land, a land flowing with milk and honey, and will give it to us.

Numbers 15:17-19   The Lord said to Moses, "Speak to the Israelites and say to them: 'When you enter the land to which I am taking you and you eat the food of the land, present a portion as an offering to the Lord.'"

Numbers 26:52-56   The Lord said to Moses, "The land is to be allotted to them as an inheritance based on the number of names. To a larger group give a larger inheritance, and to a smaller group a smaller one; each is to receive its inheritance according to the number of those listed. Be sure that the land is distributed by lot. What each group inherits will be according to the names for its ancestral tribe. Each inheritance is to be distributed by lot among the larger and smaller groups."

Numbers 27:12   Then the Lord said to Moses, "Go up this mountain in the Abarim range and see the land I have given the Israelites."

Numbers 32:7   Why do you discourage the Israelites from going over into the land the Lord has given them?

Numbers 32:22   Then when the land is subdued before the Lord, you may return and be free from your obligation to the Lord and to Israel. And this land will be your possession before the Lord.

Numbers 33:51-54   Speak to the Israelites and say to them: "When you cross the Jordan into Canaan, drive out all the inhabitants of the land before you. Destroy all their carved images and their cast idols, and demolish all their high places. Take possession of the land and settle in it, for I have given you the land to possess. Distribute the land by lot, according to your clans. To a larger group give a larger inheritance, and to a smaller group a smaller one. Whatever falls to them by lot will be theirs. Distribute it according to your ancestral tribes."

Numbers Chapter 34   (Boundaries of Canaan)

Numbers 36:7-9   No inheritance in Israel is to pass from tribe to tribe, for every Israelite shall keep the tribal land inherited from his forefathers. Every daugher who inherits land in any Israelite tribe must marry someone in her father's tribal clan, so that every Israelite will possess the inheritance of his fathers. No inheritance may pass from tribe to tribe, for each Israelite tribe is to keep the land it inherits.

Deuteronomy 1:8　See, I have given you this land. Go in and take possession of the land that the Lord swore he would give to your fathers — to Abraham, Isaac and Jacob — and to their descendants after them.

Deuteronomy 1:21　See, the Lord your God has given you the land. Go up and take possession of it as the Lord, the God of your fathers, told you. Do not be afraid; do not be discouraged.

Deuteronomy 1:25　Taking with them some of the fruit of the land, they brought it down to us and reported, "It is a good land that the Lord our God is giving us."

Deuteronomy 1:38,39　But your assistant, Joshua son of Nun, will enter it. Encourage him, because he will lead Israel to inherit it. And the little ones that you said would be taken captive, your children who do not yet know good from bad — they will enter the land. I will give it to them and they will take possession of it.

Deuteronomy 3:28　But commission Joshua, and encourage and strengthen him, for he will lead this people across and will cause them to inherit the land that you will see.

Deuteronomy 4:1　Hear now, O Israel, the decrees and laws I am about to teach you. Follow then so that you may live and may go in and take possession of the land that the Lord, the God of your fathers, is giving you.

Deuteronomy 4:5,6　See, I have taught you decrees and laws as the Lord my God commanded me, so that you may follow them in the land you are entering to take possession of it. Observe them carefully, for this will show your wisdom and understanding to the nations, who will hear about all these decrees and say, "Surely this great nation is a wise and understanding people."

Deuteronomy 4:14　And the Lord directed me at that time to teach you the decrees and laws you are to follow in the land that you are crossing the Jordan to possess.

Deuteronomy 4:22,23,24　I will die in this land; I will not cross the Jordan; but you are about to cross over and take possession of that good land. Be careful not to forget the covenant of the Lord your God that he made with you; do not make for yourselves an idol in the form of anything the Lord your God has forbidden.

Deuteronomy 4:27-31 The Lord will scatter you among the peoples, and only a few of you will survive among the nations to which the Lord will drive you. There you will worship manmade gods of wood and stone, which cannot see or hear or eat or smell. But if from there you seek the Lord your God, you will find him if you look for him with all your heart and with all your soul. When you are in distress and all these things have happened to you, then in later days you will return to the Lord your God and obey him. For the Lord your God is a merciful God; he will not abandon or destroy you or forget the covenant with your forefathers, which he confirmed to them by oath.

Deuteronomy 4:32-38 Ask now about the former days, long before your time, from the day God created man on the earth; ask from one end of the heavens to the other. Has anything so great as this ever happened, or has anything like it ever been heard of? Has any other people heard the voice of God speaking out of fire, as you have, and lived? Has any god ever tried to take for himself one nation out of another nation, by testings, by miraculous signs and wonders, by war, by a mighty hand and an outstretched arm, or by great and awesome deeds, like all the things the Lord your God did for you in Egypt before your very eyes? You were shown these things so that you might know that the Lord is God; besides him there is no other. From heaven he made you hear his voice to discipline you. On earth he showed you his great fire, and you heard his words from out of the fire. Because he loved your forefathers and chose their descendants after them, he brought you out of Egypt by his Presence and his great strength, to drive out before you nations greater and stronger than you and *to bring you into their land to give it to you for your inheritance, as it is today.*

Deuteronomy 4:39,40 Acknowledge and take to heart this day that the Lord is God in heaven above and on the earth below. There is no other. Keep his decrees and commands, which I am giving you today, so that it may go well with you and your children after you and *that you may live long in the land the Lord your God gives you for all time.*

Deuteronomy 5:32,33 So be careful to do what the Lord your God has commanded you; do not turn aside to the right or to the left. Walk in all the way that the Lord your God has commanded you, so that you may live and prosper and prolong your days in the land that you will possess.

Deuteronomy 6:3   Hear, O Israel, and be careful to obey so that it may go well with you and that you may increase greatly in a land flowing with milk and honey, just as the Lord, the God of your fathers, promised you.

Deuteronomy 6:10-12   When the Lord your God brings you into the land he swore to your fathers, to Abraham, Isaac and Jacob, to give you — a land with large, flourishing cities you did not build, houses filled with all kinds of good things you did not provide, wells you did not dig, and vineyards and olive groves you did not plant — then when you eat and are satisfied, be careful that you do not forget the Lord, who brought you out of Egypt, out of the land of slavery.

Deuteronomy 6:18   Do what is right and good in the Lord's sight, so that it may go well with you and you may go in and take over the good land that the Lord promised on oath to your forefathers.

Deuteronomy 6:23   But he brought us out from there to bring us in and give us the land that he promised on oath to our forefathers.

Deuteronomy 7:7-9   The Lord did not set his affection on you and choose you because you were more numerous than other peoples, for you were the fewest of all peoples. But it was because the Lord loved you and kept the oath he swore to your forefathers that he brought you out with a mighty hand and redeemed you from the land of slavery, from the power of Pharaoh king of Egypt. Know therefore that the Lord your God is God; he is the faithful God, keeping his covenant of love to a thousand generations of those who love him and keep his commands.

Deuteronomy 7:12,13   If you pay attention to these laws and are careful to follow them then the Lord your God will keep his covenant of love with you, as he swore to your forefathers. He will love you and bless you and increase your numbers. He will bless the fruit of your womb, the crops of your land — your grain, new wine and oil — the calves of your herds and the lambs of your flocks in the land that he swore to your forefathers to give you.

Deuteronomy 8:1   Be careful to follow every command I am giving you today, so that you may live and increase and may enter and possess the land that the Lord promised on oath to your forefathers.

Deuteronomy 8:6-9   Observe the commands of the Lord your God, walking in his ways and revering him. For the Lord your God is bringing you into a good land — a land with streams and pools of water, with springs flowing in the valleys and hills, a land with wheat and barley, vines and fig trees, pomegranates, olive oil and honey; a land where bread will not be scarce and you will lack nothing; a land where the rocks are iron and you can dig copper out of the hills.

Deuteronomy 8:10   When you have eaten and are satisfied, praise the Lord your God for the good land he has given you.

Deuteronomy 8:18   But remember the Lord your God, for it is he who gives you the ability to produce wealth, and so *confirms his covenant*, which he swore to your forefathers, as it is today.

Deuteronomy 9:1   Hear, O Israel. You are now about to cross the Jordan to go in and dispossess nations greater and stronger than you, with large cities that have walls up to the sky.

Deuteronomy 9:5   It is not because of your righteousness or your integrity that you are going in to take possession of their land; but on account of the wickedness of these nations.

Deuteronomy 10:11   "Go," the Lord said to me, "and lead the people on their way, so that they may enter and possess the land that I swore to their fathers to give them."

Deuteronomy 11:8,9   Observe therefore all the commands I am giving you today, so that you may have the strength to go in and take over the land that you are crossing the Jordan to possess, and so that you may live long in the land that the Lord swore to your forefathers to give to them and their descendants, a land flowing with milk and honey.

Deuteronomy 11:10-12   The land you are entering to take over is not like the land of Egypt, from which you have come, where you planted your seed and irrigated it by foot as in a vegetable garden. But the land you are crossing the Jordan to take possession of is a land of mountains and valleys that drinks rain from heaven. It is a land the Lord your God cares for; the eyes of the Lord your God are continually on it from the beginning of the year to its end.

Deuteronomy 11:18-21   Fix these words of mine in your hearts and minds; tie them as symbols on your hands and bind them on your foreheads. Teach them to your children, talking about them when you sit at home and when you walk along the road, when you lie down and when you get up. Write them on the doorframes of your houses and on your gates, so that your days and the days of your children may be many in the land that the Lord swore to give your forefathers, as many as the days that the heavens are above the earth.

Deuteronomy 11:24   Every place where you set your foot will be yours; from the desert to Lebanon, and from the Euphrates River to the western sea.

Deuteronomy 11:31,32   You are about to cross the Jordan to enter and take possession of the land the Lord your God is giving you. When you have taken it over and are living there, be sure that you obey all the decrees and laws I am setting before you today.

Deuteronomy 15:4-6   However, there should be no poor among you, for in the land the Lord your God is giving you to possess as your inheritance, he will richly bless you, if only you fully obey the Lord your God and are careful to follow all these commands I am giving you today. For the Lord your God will bless you as he has promised, and you will lend to many nations but will borrow from none. You will rule over many nations but none will rule over you.

Deuteronomy 16:20   Follow justice and justice alone, so that you may live and possess the land the Lord your God is giving you.

Deuteronomy 17:14,15   When you enter the land the Lord your God is giving you and have taken possession of it and settled in it, and you say, "Let us set a king over us like all the nations around us," be sure to appoint over you the king the Lord your God chooses. He must be from among your own brothers. Do not place a foreigner over you, one who is not a brother Israelite.

Deuteronomy 18:9   When you enter the land the Lord your God is giving you, do not learn to imitate the detestable ways of the nations there.

Deuteronomy 26:1-3   When you have entered the land the Lord your God is giving you as an inheritance and have taken possession of it and settled in it, take some of the firstfruits of all that you produce from the soil of the land the Lord your God is giving you and put them in a basket. Then go to the place the Lord your God will choose as a dwelling for his Name and say to the priest in office at the time, "I declare today to the Lord your God that I have come to the land the Lord swore to our forefathers to give us."

Deuteronomy 26:15   Look down from heaven, your holy dwelling place, and bless your people Israel and the land you have given us as you promised an oath to our forefathers, a land flowing with milk and honey.

Deuteronomy 27:3   Write on them all the words of this law when you have crossed over to enter the land the Lord your God is giving you, a land flowing with milk and honey, just as the Lord, the God of your fathers, promised you.

Deuteronomy 28:8   The Lord will send a blessing on your barns and on everything you put your hand to. The Lord your God will bless you in the land he is giving you.

Deuteronomy 26:18,19   And the Lord has declared this day that you are his people, his treasured possession as he promised, and that you are to keep all his commands. He has declared that he will set you in praise, fame and honor high above all the nations he has made and that you will be a people holy to the Lord your God, as he promised.

Deuteronomy 28:9-11   The Lord will establish you as his holy people, as he promised you on oath, if you keep the commands of the Lord your God and walk in his ways. Then all the peoples on earth will see that you are called by the name of the Lord, and they will fear you. The Lord will grant you abundant prosperity — in the fruit of your womb, the young of your livestock and the crops of your ground — in the land he swore to your forefathers to give you.

Deuteronomy 30:1-5   When all these blessings and curses I have set before you come upon you and you take them to heart wherever the Lord your God disperses you among the nations, and when you and your children return to the Lord your God and obey him with all your heart and with all your soul according to everything I command you today, then the Lord your God will restore your fortunes and have compassion on you and gather you again from all the nations where he scattered you. Even if you have been banished to the most distant land under the heavens, from there the Lord your God will gather you and bring you back. He will bring you to the land that belonged to your fathers, and you will take possession of it. He will make you more prosperous and numerous than your fathers.

Deuteronomy 30:19,20   This day I call heaven and earth as witnesses against you that I have set before you life and death, blessings and curses. Now choose life, so that you and your children may live and that you may love the Lord your God, listen to his voice, and hold fast to him. For the Lord is your life, and he will give you many years in the land he swore to give to your fathers, Abraham, Isaac and Jacob.

Deuteronomy 31:3   The Lord your God himself will cross over ahead of you. He will destroy these nations before you, and you will take possession of their land. Joshua also will cross over ahead of you, as the Lord said.

Deuteronomy 31:7   Then Moses summoned Joshua and said to him in the presence of all Israel, "Be strong and courageous, for you must go with this people into the land that the Lord swore to their forefathers to give them, and you must divide it among them as their inheritance."

Deuteronomy 31:19-22   "Now write down for yourselves this song and teach it to the Israelites and have them sing it, so that it may be a witness for me against them. When I have brought them into the land flowing with milk and honey, the land I promised on oath to their forefathers, and when they eat their fill and thrive, they will turn to other gods and worship them, rejecting me and breaking my covenant. And when many disasters and difficulties come upon them, this song will testify against them, because it will not be forgotten by their descendants. I know what they are disposed to do, even before I bring them into the land I promised them on oath." So Moses wrote down this song that day and taught it to the Israelites!

Deuteronomy 31:23   The Lord gave this command to Joshua son of Nun: "Be strong and courageous, for you will bring the Israelites into the land I promised them on oath, and I myself will be with you."

Deuteronomy 32:45-47   When Moses finished reciting all these words to all Israel, he said to them, "Take to heart all the words I have solemnly declared to you this day, so that you may command your children to obey carefully all the words of this law. They are not just idle words for you — they are your life. By them you will live long in the land you are crossing the Jordan to possess.

Deuteronomy 32:48,49   On that same day the Lord told Moses, "Go up into the Abarim Range to Mount Nebo in Moab, across from Jericho, and view Canaan, the land I am giving the Israelites as their own possession."

Deuteronomy 34:1-4   Then Moses climbed Mount Nebo from the plains of Moab to the top of Pisgah, across from Jericho. There the Lord showed him the whole land — from Gilead to Dan, all of Naphtali, the territory of Ephraim and Manasseh, all the land of Judah as far as the western sea, the Negev and the whole region from the valley of Jericho, the City of Palms, as far as Zoar. Then the Lord said to him, "This is the land I promised on oath to Abraham, Isaac and Jacob when I said, 'I will give it to your descendants.' I have let you see it with your eyes, but you will not cross over into it.' "

Joshua 1:2-6   Moses my servant is dead. Now then, you and all these people, get ready to cross the Jordan River into the land I am about to give to them — to the Israelites. I will give you every place where you set your foot, as I promised Moses. Your territory will extend from the desert and from Lebanon to the great river, the Euphrates — all the Hittite country — and to the Great Sea on the west. No one will be able to stand up against you all the days of your life. As I was with Moses, so I will be with you; I will never leave you nor forsake you. Be strong and courageous, because you will lead these people to inherit the land I swore to their forefathers to give them.

Joshua 1:15   Until the Lord gives them rest, as he has done for you, and until they too have taken possession of the land that the Lord your God is giving them.

Joshua 2:24   They said to Joshua, "The Lord has surely given the whole land into our hands; all the people are melting in fear because of us."

Joshua 5:10-12   On the evening of the fourteenth day of the month, while camped at Gilgal on the plains of Jericho, the Israelites celebrated the Passover. The day after the Passover, that very day, they ate some of the produce of the land: unleavened bread and roasted grain. The manna stopped the day after they ate this food from the land; there was no longer any manna for the Israelites, but that year they ate of the produce of Canaan.

Joshua 11:16,17   So Joshua took this entire land: the hill country, all the Negev, the whole region of Goshen, the western foothills, the Arabah and the mountains of Israel with their foothills, from Mount Halak, which rises toward Seir, to Baal Gad in the Valley of Lebanon below Mount Hermon. He captures all their kings and struck them down, putting them to death.

Joshua 11:23   So Joshua took the entire land, just as the Lord had directed Moses, and he gave it as an inheritance to Israel according to their tribal division. Then the land had rest from war.

Joshua 14:13,14   Then Joshua blessed Caleb son of Jephunneh and gave him Hebron as his inheritance. So Hebron has belonged to Caleb son of Jephunneh the Kennizzite ever since, because he followed the Lord, the God of Israel, wholeheartedly.

Joshua Chapters 13 through 19   Describes the allocation of territories to the tribes of Israel.

Joshua 22:4   Now that the Lord your God has given your brothers rest as he promised, return to your homes in the land that Moses the servant of the Lord gave you on the other side of the Jordan.

Joshua 22:8   When Joshua sent them home, he blessed them, saying, "Return to your homes with your great wealth — with large herds of livestock, with silver, gold, bronze and iron, and a great quantity of clothing — and divide with your brothers the plunder from your enemies."

Joshua 24:13   So I gave you a land on which you did not toil and cities you did not build; and you live in them and eat from vineyards and olive groves that you did not plant.

Joshua 24:29,32   (Joseph buried in the promised land with rest of Patriarchs)

Judges 1:1,2   After the death of Joshua, the Israelites asked the Lord, "Who will be the first to go up and fight for us against the Canaanites?" The Lord answered, "Judah is to go; I have given the land into their hands."

Judges 2:1   The Angel of the Lord went up from Gilgal to Bokim and said, "I brought you up out of Egypt and led you into the land that I swore to give to your forefathers. I said, 'I will never break my covenant with you.'"

Ruth 1:7   With her two daughters-in-law she left the place where she had been living and set out on the road that would take them back to the land of Judah.

I Samuel 22:5   But the prophet Gad said to David, "Do not stay in the stronghold. Go into the land of Judah."

II Samuel 7:10   And I will provide a place for my people Israel and will plant them so that they can have a home of their own and no longer be disturbed. Wicked people will not oppress them anymore, as they did at the beginning.

II Chronicles 30:9   If you return to the Lord, then your brothers and your children will be shown compassion by their captors and will come back to this land, for the Lord your God is gracious and compassionate. He will not turn His face from you if you return to him.

Ezra 10:7   A proclamation was then issued throughout Judah and Jerusalem for all the exiles to assemble in Jerusalem.

Ezra Chapter 8   (Return to Jerusalem from Babylonian captivity and bringing the wealth back to Jerusalem.)

Nehemiah 1:8,9   Remember the instruction you gave your servant

Moses, saying, "If you are unfaithful, I will scatter you among the nations, but if you return to me and obey my commands, then even if your exiled people are at the farthest horizon, I will gather them from there and bring them to the place I have chosen as a dwelling for my Name."

Nehemiah Chapter 7   (The list of exiles who returned from the Babylonian Captivity.)

Nehemiah 7:66,67   The whole company numbered 42,360, besides their 7,337 menservants and maidservants; and they also had 245 men and women singers.

Nehemiah 9:7,8   You are the Lord God, who chose Abram and brought him out of Ur of the Chaldeans and named him Abraham. You found his heart faithful to you, and you made a covenant with him to give to his descendants the land of the Canaanites, Hittites, Amorites, Perizzites, Jebusites and Girgashites. You have kept your promise because your are righteous.

Nehemiah 9:23-25   You made their sons as numerous as the stars in the sky, and you brought them into the land that you told their fathers to enter and possess. Their sons went in and took possession of the land. You subdued before them the Canaanites, who lived in the land; you handed the Canaanites over to them, along with their kings and the peoples of the land, to deal with them as they pleased. They captured fortified cities and fertile land; they took possession of houses filled with all kinds of good things, wells already dug, vineyards, olive groves and fruit trees in abundance. They ate to the full and were well nourished; they reveled in your great goodness.

Psalm 2:8   Ask of me, and I will make the nations your inheritance, the ends of the earth your possession.

Psalm 14:7   Oh, that salvation for Israel would come out of Zion! When the Lord restores the fortunes of his people, let Jacob rejoice and Israel be glad!

Psalm 25:13   He will spend his days in prosperity, and his descendants will inherit the land.

Psalm 27:4   One thing I ask of the Lord, this is what I seek: that I may dwell in the house of the Lord all the days of my life, to gaze upon the beauty of the Lord and to seek him in his temple.

Psalm 33:12   Blessed is the nation whose God is the Lord, the people he chose for his inheritance.

Psalm 37:3   Trust in the Lord and do good; dwell in the land and enjoy safe pasture.

Psalm 37:11   But the meek will inherit the land and enjoy great peace.

Psalm 37:22   Those the Lord blesses will inherit the land, but those he curses will be cut off.

Psalm 37:29   The righteous will inherit the land and dwell in it forever.

Psalm 37:34   Wait for the Lord and keep his way. He will exalt you to possess the land; when the wicked are cut off, you will see it.

Psalm 53:6   Oh, that salvation for Israel would come out of Zion! When God restores the fortunes of his people, let Jacob rejoice and Israel be glad!

Psalm 69:33-36   The Lord hears the needy and does not despise his captive people. Let heaven and earth praise him, the seas and all that move in them, for God will save Zion and rebuild the cities of Judah. Then people will settle there and possess it; the children of his servants will inherit it, and those who love his name will dwell there.

Psalm 74:2   Remember the people you purchased of old, the tribe you redeemed as your inheritance — Mount Zion, where you dwelt.

Psalm 77:14,15   You are the God who performs miracles; you display your power among the peoples. With you mighty arm you redeemed your people, the descendants of Jacob and Joseph.

Psalm 78:54,55   Thus he brought them to the border of his holy land, to the hill country his right hand had taken. He drove out nations before them and allotted their lands to them as an inheritance; he settled the tribes of Israel in their homes.

Psalm 84:10   Better is one day in your courts than a thousand elsewhere; I would rather be a doorkeeper in the house of my God than dwell in the tents of the wicked.

Psalm 85:1   You showed favor to your land, O Lord; you restored the fortunes of Jacob.

Psalm 85:12   The Lord will indeed give what is good, and our land will yield its harvest.

Psalm 87:1,2   He has set his foundation on the holy mountain; the Lord loves the gates of Zion more than all the dwellings of Jacob.

Psalm 94:14   For the Lord will not reject his people: he will never forsake his inheritance.

Psalm 105:6-11   O descendants of Abraham his servant, O sons of Jacob, his chosen ones. He is the Lord our God; his judgments are in all the earth. He remembers his covenant forever, the word he commanded, for a thousand generations, the covenant he made with Abraham, the oath he swore to Isaac. He confirmed it to Jacob as a decree, to Israel as an everlasting covenant: "To you I will give the land of Canaan as the portion you will inherit."

Psalm 105:37   He brought out Israel, laden with silver and gold, and from among their tribes no one faltered.

Psalm 105:42-45   For he remembered his holy promise given to his servant Abraham. He brought out his people with rejoicing, his chosen ones with shouts of joy; he gave them the lands of the nations, and they fell heir to what others had toiled for — that they might keep his precepts and observe his laws. Praise the Lord!

Psalm 106:47   Save us, O Lord our God, and gather us from the nations, that we may give thanks to your holy name and glory in your praise.

Psalm 107:2,3   Let the redeemed of the Lord say this — those he redeemed from the hand of the foe, those he gathered from the lands, from east and west, from north and south.

Psalm 107;7,9   He led them by a straight way to a city where they could settle.

Psalm 107:36-38   There he brought the hungry to live, and they founded a city where they could settle. They sowed fields and planted vineyards that yielded a fruitful harvest; he blessed them, and their numbers greatly increased, and he did not let their herds diminish.

Psalm 111:4-6   He provides food for those who fear him; he remembers his covenant forever. He has shown his people the power of his works, giving them the lands of other nations.

Psalm 114:1,2   When Israel came out of Egypt, the house of Jacob freom a people of foreign tongue, Judah became God's sanctuary, Israel his dominion.

Psalm 121:4   Indeed, he who watches over Israel will neither slumber nor sleep.

Psalm 122:1-4   I rejoiced with those who said to me, "Let us go to the house of the Lord." Our feet are standing in your gates, O Jerusalem. Jerusalem is built like a city that is closely compacted together. That is where the tribes go up, the tribes of the Lord, to praise the name of the Lord according to the statute given to Israel.

Psalm 125:2   As the mountains surround Jerusalem, so the Lord surrounds his people both now and forevermore.

Psalm 126   When the Lord brought back the captives to Zion, we were like men who dreamed. Our mouths were filled with laughter, our tongues with songs of joy. Then it was said among the nations, "The Lord has done great things for them" The Lord has done great things for us, and we are filled with joy. Restore our fortunes, O Lord, like streams in the Negev. Those who sow in tears will reap with songs of joy. He who goes out weeping, carrying seed to sow, will return with songs of joy, carrying sheaves with him.

Psalm 127:1   Unless the Lord builds the house, its builders labor in vain. Unless the Lord watches over the city, the watchmen stand guard in vain.

Psalm 128:5,6   May the Lord bless you from Zion all the days of your life; may you see the prosperity of Jerusalem, and may you live to see your children's children. Peace be upon Israel.

Psalm 130:7,8   O Israel, put your hope in the Lord, for with the Lord is unfailing love and with him is full redemption. He himself will redeem Israel from all their sins.

Psalm 135;4   For the Lord has chosen Jacob to be his own, Israel to be his treasured possession.

Psalm 135:12   And he gave their land as an inheritance, an inheritance to his people Israel.

Psalm 136:21   And gave their land as an inheritance, His love endures forever, an inheritance to his servant Israel; His love endures forever.

Psalm 137:4-6   How can we sing the songs of the Lord while in a foreign land? If I forget you, O Jerusalem, may my right hand forget its skill. May my tongue cling to the roof of my mouth if I do not remember you, if I do not consider Jerusalem my highest joy.

Psalm 147:2,3   The Lord builds up Jerusalem; he gathers the exiles of Israel. He heals the brokenhearted and binds up their wounds.

Isaiah 10:21,22   A remnant will return, a remnant of Jacob will return to the Mighty God. Though your people, O Israel, be like the sand by the sea, only a remnant will return.

Isaiah 11:11,12   In that day the Lord will reach out his hand a second time to reclaim the remnant that is left of his people from Assyria, from Lower Egypt, from Upper Egypt, from Cush, from Elam, from Babylonia, from Hamath and from the islands of the sea. He will raise a banner for the nations and gather the exiles of Israel; He will assemble the scattered people of Judah from the four quarters of the earth.

Isaiah 14:1,2   The Lord will have compassion on Jacob; (Israel) once again he will choose Israel and will settle them in their own land. Aliens will join them and unite with the house of Jacob. Nations will take them and bring them to their own place. And the house of Israel will possess the nations as menservants and maidservants in the Lord's land.

Isaiah 27:12,13   In that day the Lord will thresh from the flowing Euphrates to the Wadi of Egypt, and you, O Israelites, will be gathered up one by one. And in that day a great trumpet will sound. Those who were perishing in Assyria and those who were exiled in Egypt will come and worship the Lord on the holy mountain in Jerusalem.

Isaiah 35:10   And the ransomed of the Lord will return. They will enter Zion with singing; everlasting joy will crown their heads. Gladness and joy will overtake them, and sorrow and sighing will flee away.

Isaiah 43:5,6   Do not be afraid, for I am with you; I will bring your children from the east and gather you from the west. I will say to the north, "Give them up!" and to the south, "Do not hold them back," Bring my sons from afar and my daughters from the ends of the earth.

Isaiah 44:21,22   Remember these things, O Jacob, for you are my servant, O Israel, I have made you, you are my servant; O Israel, I will not forget you. I have swept away your offenses like a cloud, your sins like the morning mist. Return to me, for I have redeemed you.

Isaiah 41:8-10   But you, O Israel, my servant, Jacob, whom I have chosen, you descendants of Abraham my friend, I took you from the ends of the earth, from its farthest corners I called you. I said, "You are my servant"; I have chosen you and have not rejected you. So do not fear, for I am with you; do not be dismayed, for I am your God. I will strengthen you and help you; I will uphold you with my righteous right hand.

Isaiah 43:16-19a   This is what the Lord says — he who made a way through the sea, a path through the mighty waters, who drew out the chariots and horses, the army and reinforcements together, and they lay there, never to rise again, extinguished, snuffed out like a wick:

Forget the former things; do not dwell on the past. See, I am doing a new thing! Now it springs up; do you not perceive it?

Isaiah 44:26   Who carries out the words of his servants and fulfills the predictions of his messengers, who says of Jerusalem, "It shall be inhabited," of the towns of Judah, "They shall be built," and of their ruins, "I will restore them."

Isaiah 45:20   Gather together and come; assemble, you fugitives from the nations.

Isaiah 46:3,4   Listen to me, O house of Jacob, all you who remain of the house of Israel, you whom I have upheld since you were conceived, and have carried since your birth. Even to your old age and gray hairs I am he, I am he who will sustain you. I have made you and I will carry you; I will sustain you and I will rescue you.

Isaiah 48:20   Leave Babylon, flee from the Babylonians! Announce this with shouts of joy and proclaim it. Send it out to the ends of the earth; say, "The Lord has redeemed his servant Jacob."

Isaiah 49:5,6   And now the Lord says — he who formed me in the womb to be his servant to bring Jacob back to him and gather Israel to himself, for I am honored in the eyes of the Lord and my God has been my strength — he says: "It is too small a thing for you to be my servant to restore the tribes of Jacob and bring back those of Israel I have kept. I will also make you a light for the Gentiles, that you may bring my salvation to the ends of the earth."

Isaiah 49:11,12   I will turn all my mountains into roads, and my highways will be raised up. See, they will come from afar — some from the north, some from the west, some from the region of Sinim.

Isaiah 49:14-18   But Zion said, "The Lord has forsaken me, the Lord has forgotten me." Can a mother forget the baby at her breast and have no compassion on the child she has borne? Though she may forget, I will not forget you! See, I have engraved you on the palms of my hands; your walls are ever before me. Your sons hasten back, and those who laid you waste depart from you. Lift up your eyes and look around; all your sons gather and come to you. "As surely as I live," declares the Lord, "You will wear them all as ornaments; you will put them on, like a bride."

Isaiah 49:19,20   Though you were ruined and made desolate and your land laid waste, now you will be too small for your people, and those who devoured you will be far away. The children born during your bereavement will yet say in your hearing, "This place is too small for us; give us more space to live in."

Isaiah 49:22 This is what the Sovereign Lord says: "See, I will beckon to the Gentiles, I will lift up my banner to the peoples; they will bring your sons in their arms and carry your daughters on their shoulders."

Isaiah 51:3 The Lord will surely comfort Zion and will look with compassion on all her ruins; he will make her deserts like Eden, her wastelands like the garden of the Lord. Joy and gladness will be found in her, thanksgiving and the sound of singing.

Isaiah 51:11 The ransomed of the Lord will return. They will enter Zion with singing; everlasting joy will crown their heads. Gladness and joy will overtake them, and sorrow and sighing will flee away.

Isaiah 52:2,3 Shake off your dust; rise up, sit enthroned, O Jerusalem. Free yourself from the chains on your neck, O captive Daughter of Zion. For this is what the Lord says: "You were sold for nothing, and without money you will be redeemed."

Isaiah 52:11,12 Depart, depart, go out from there! Touch no unclean thing. Come out from it and be pure, you who carry the vessels of the Lord. But you will not leave in haste or go in flight; for the Lord will go before you, The God of Israel will be your rear guard.

Isaiah 54:3 For you will spread out to the right and to the left; your descendants will dispossess nations and settle in their desolate cities.

Isaiah 54:6-8 "The Lord will call you back as if you were a wife deserted and distressed in spirit — a wife who married young, only to be rejected," says your God. "For a brief moment I abandoned you, but with deep compassion I will bring you back. In a surge of anger I hid my face from you for a moment, but with everlasting kindness I will have compassion on you," says the Lord your Redeemer.

Isaiah 56:6-8 And foreigners who bind themselves to the Lord to serve him, to love the name of the Lord, and to worship him, all who keep the Sabbath without desecrating it and who hold fast to my covenant — these I will bring to my holy mountain and give them joy in my house of prayer. Their burnt offerings and sacrifices will be accepted on my altar; for my house will be called a house of prayer for all nations. The Sovereign Lord declares — he who gathers the exiles of Israel; "I will gather still others to them besides those already gathered."

Isaiah 57:13   When you cry out for help, let your collection of idols save you! The wind will carry all of them off, a mere breath will blow them away. But the man who makes me his refuge will inherit the land and possess my holy mountain.

Isaiah 58:12   Your people will rebuild the ancient ruins and will raise up the age-old foundations; you will be called Repairer of Broken Walls, Restorer of Streets with Dwellings.

Isaiah 58:14   "Then you will find your joy in the Lord, and I will cause you to ride on the heights of the land and to feast on the inheritance of your father Jacob." The mouth of the Lord has spoken.

Isaiah 60:4,5   Lift up your eyes and look about you; All assemble and come to you; your sons come from afar, and your daughers are carried on the arm. Then you will look and be radiant, your heart will throb and swell within you; the wealth on the seas will be brought to you, to you the riches of the nations will come.

Isaiah 61:4-7   They will rebuild the ancient ruins and restore the places long devastated; they will renew the ruined cities that have been devastated for generations. Aliens will shepherd your flocks; foreigners will work your fields and vineyards. And you will be called priests of the Lord, you will be named ministers of our God. You will feed on the wealth of nations, and in their riches you will boast. Instead of their shame my people will recieve a double portion, and instead of disgrace they will rejoice in their inheritance; and so they will inherit a double portion in their land, and everlasting joy will be theirs.

Isaiah 62   For Zion's sake I will not keep silent, for Jerusalem's sake I will not remain quiet, till her righteousness shines out like the dawn, her salvation like a blazing torch. The nations will see your righteousness, and all kings your glory; you will be called by a new name that the mouth of the Lord will bestow. You will be a crown of splendor in the Lord's hand, a royal diadem in the hand of your God. No longer will they call you Deserted, or name your land Desolate. But you will be called Hephzibah, and your land Beulah; for the Lord will take delight in you, and your land will be married. As a young man marries a maiden, so will your sons marry you; as a bridegroom rejoices over his bride, so will your God rejoice over you. I have posted watchmen on your walls, O Jerusalem; they will never be silent day or night. You who call on the Lord, give yourselves no rest, and give him no rest till he establishes Jerusalem and makes her the praise of the earth. The Lord has sworn by his right hand and by his mighty arm: "Never again will I give your grain as food for your enemies, and never again will foreigners drink the new wine for which you have toiled; but those who harvest it will eat it and praise the Lord, and those who gather the grapes will drink it in the courts of my sanctuary." Pass through, pass through the gates! Prepare the way for the people. Build up, build up the highway! Remove the stones. Raise a banner for the nations. The Lord has made proclamation to the ends of the earth: Say to the Daughter of Zion, See, your Savior comes! See, his recompense accompanies him.' " They will be called The Holy People, The Redeemed of the Lord; and you will be called Sought After, The City No Longer Deserted.

Isaiah 63:17,18   Why, O Lord, do you make us wander from your ways and harden our hearts so we do not revere you? Return for the sake of your servants, the tribes that are your inheritance. For a little while your people possessed your holy place, but now our enemies have trampled down your sanctuary.

Isaiah 65:9,10   I will bring forth descendants from Jacob, and from Judah those who will possess my mountains, my chosen people will inherit them, and there will my servants live.

Isaiah 66:8-10   Who has ever heard of such a thing? Who has ever seen such things? Can a country be born in a day or a nation be brought forth in a moment? Yet no sooner is Zion in labor than she gives birth to her children. Do I bring to the moment of birth and not give delivery?" says the Lord. Do I close up the womb when I bring to delivery?" says your God. Rejoice with Jerusalem and be glad for her, all you who love her, rejoice greatly with her, all you who mourn over her.

Isaiah 66:18   And I, because of their actions and their imaginations, am about to come and gather all nations and tongues, and they will come and see my glory.

Isaiah 66:20-22   "And they will bring all your brothers, from all the nations to my holy mountain in Jerusalem as an offering to the Lord — on horses, in chariots and wagons, and on mules and camels," says the Lord. "They will bring them, as the Israelites bring their grain offerings to the temple of the Lord in ceremonially clean vessels." And I will select some of them also to be priests and Levites," says the Lord. "As the new heavens and the new earth that I made will endure before me," declares the Lord, "so will your name and descendants endure."

Jeremiah 3:14-18   "Return, faithless people," declares the Lord, "for I am your husband. I will choose one of you from every town and two from every clan and bring you to Zion. Then I will give you shepherds after my own heart, who will lead you with knowledge and understanding. In those days, when your numbers have increased greatly in the land," declares the Lord, "men will no longer say, 'The ark of the covenant of the Lord.'" It will never enter their minds or be remembered; it will not be missed, nor will another one be made. At that time they will call Jerusalem The Throne of the Lord, and all nations will gather in Jerusalem to honor the name of the Lord. No longer will they follow the stubbornness of their evil hearts. In those days the house of Judah will join the house of Israel, and together they will come from a northern land to the land I gave your forefathers as an inheritance.

Jeremiah 4:5,6 Announce in Judah and proclaim in Jerusalem and say: "Sound the trumpet throughout the land!" Cry aloud and say: "Gather together! Let us flee to the fortified cities!" Raise the signal to go to Zion! Flee for safety without delay! For I am bringing disaster from the north, even terrible destruction.

Jeremiah 12:14,15 This is what the Lord says: "As for all my wicked neighbors who seize the inheritance I gave my people Israel, I will uproot them from their lands and I will uproot the house of Judah from among them. But after I uproot them, I will again have compassion and will bring each of them back to his own inheritance and his own country."

Jeremiah 16:14,15 "However, the days ar coming," declares the Lord, "when men will no longer say, 'As surely as the Lord lives, who brought the Israelites up out of Egypt,' but they will say, 'As surely as the Lord lives, who brought the Israelites up out of the land of the north and out of all the countries where he had banished them.' For I will restore them to the land I gave their forefathers."

Jeremiah 23:3-6 "I myself will gather the remnant of my flock out of all the countries where I have driven them and will bring them back to their pasture, where they will be fruitful and increase in number. I will place shepherds over them who will tend them, and they will no longer be afraid of terrified, nor will any be missing," declares the Lord. "The days are coming," declares the Lord, "when I will raise up to David a righteous Branch, a King who will reign wisely and do what is just and right in the land. In his days Judah will be saved and Israel will live in safety. This is the name by which he will be called: They Lord Our Righteousness."

Jeremiah 23:7,8 "So then, the days are coming," declares the Lord, "when people will no longer say, 'As surely as the Lord lives, who brought the Israelites up out of Egypt,' but they will say, 'As surely as the Lord lives, who brought the descendants of Israel up out the land of the north and out of all the countries where he had banished them.' Then they will live in their own land."

Jeremiah 24:6,7 My eyes will watch over them for their good, and I will bring them back to this land. I will build them up and not tear them down; I will plant them and not uproot them. I will give them a heart to know me, that I am the Lord. They will be my people, and I will be their God, for they will return to me with all their heart.

Jeremiah 27:22 "They will be taken to Babylon and there they will remain until the day I come for them," declares the Lord. "Then I will bring them back and restore them to this place."

Jeremiah 29:11-14 "For I know the plans I have for you," declares the Lord, "plans to prosper you and not to harm you, plans to give you hope and a future. Then you will call upon me and come and pray to me, and I will listen to you. You will seek me and find me when you seek me with all your heart. I will be found by you," declares the Lord, "and will bring you back from captivity. I will gather you from all the nations and places where I have banished you," declares the Lord, "and will bring you back to the place from which I carried you into exile."

Jeremiah 30:3 "The days are coming," declares the Lord, "when I will bring my people Israel and Judah back from captivity and restore them to the land I gave their forefathers to possess," says the Lord.

Jeremiah 30:10 "So do not fear, O Jacob my servant; do not be dismayed, O Israel," declares the Lord, "I will surely save you out of a distant place, your descendants from the land of their exile. Jacob will again have peace and security, and no one will make him afraid."

Jeremiah 31:8,9 See, I will bring them from the land of the north and gather them from the ends of the earth. Among them will be the blind and the lame, expectant mothers and women in labor; a great throne will return. They will come with weeping; they will pray as I bring them back. I will lead them beside streams of water on a level path where they will not stumble, because I am Israel's father, and Ephraim is my firstborn son.

Jeremiah 31:10,11   Hear the word of the Lord, O nations; proclaim it in distant coastlands; He who scattered Israel will gather them and will watch over his flock like a shepherd. For the Lord will ransom Jacob and redeem them from the hand of those stronger than they.

Jeremiah 31:12   They will come and shout for joy on the heights of Zion; They will rejoice in the bounty of the Lord — the grain, the new wine and the oil, the young of the flocks and herds. They will be like a well-watered garden, and they will sorrow no more.

Jeremiah 31:15-17   This is what the Lord says: "A voice is heard in Ramah mourning and great weeping, Rachel weeping for her children and refusing to be comforted because her children are no more." This is what the Lord says: "Restrain your voice from weeping and your eyes from tears, for your work will be rewarded," declares the Lord. "They will return from the land of the enemy. So there is hope for your future," declares the Lord. "Your children will return to their own land."

Jeremiah 31:21,22   Set up road signs; put up guideposts. Take note of the highway, the road that you take. Return, O Virgin Israel, return to your towns. How long will you wander, O unfaithful daughter?

Jeremiah 31:23-25   This is what the Lord Almighty, the God of Israel, says: "When I bring them back from captivity, the people in the land of Judah and in its towns will once again use these words: 'The Lord bless you, O righteous dwelling, O sacred mountain.' People will live together in Judah and all its towns — farmers and those who move about with their flocks. I will refresh the weary and satisfy the faint."

Jeremiah 31:27,28   "The days are coming," declares the Lord, "when I will plant the house of Israel and the house of Judah with the off-spring of men and of animals. Just as I watched over them to uproot and tear down, and to overthrow, destroy and bring disaster, so I will watch over them to build and to plant," declares the Lord.

Jeremiah 32:37-41   I will surely gather them from all the lands where I banish them in my furious anger and great wrath; I will bring them back to this place and let them live in safety. They will be my people, and I will be their God. I will give them singleness of heart and action, so that they will always fear me for their own good and the good of their children after them. I will make an everlasting covenant with them: I will never stop doing good to them, and I will inspire them to fear me, so that they will never turn away from me. I will rejoice in doing them good and will assuredly plant them in this land with all my heart and soul.

Jeremiah 33:7 I will bring Judah and Israel back from captivity and will rebuild them as they were before.

Jeremiah 33:14 "The days are coming," declares the Lord, "when I will fulfill the gracious promise I made to the house of Israel and to the house of Judah."

Jeremiah 46:16 They will stumble repeatedly; they will fall over each other. They will say, "Get up, let us go back to our own people and our native lands, away from the sword of the oppressor."

Jeremiah 48:27 Do not fear, O Jacob my servant; do not be dismayed, O Israel. I will surely save you out of a distant place, your descendants from the land of their exile. Jacob will again have peace and security, and no one will make him afraid.

Jeremiah 50:3-5 A nation from the north will attack her and lay waste her land. No one will live in it; both men and animals will flee away. "In those days, at that time," declares the Lord, "the people of Israel and the people of Judah together will go in tears to seek the Lord their God. They will ask the way to Zion and turn their faces toward it. They will come and bind themselves to the Lord in an everlasting covenant that will not be forgotten."

Jeremiah 50:19 But I will bring Israel back to his own pasture and he will graze on Carmel and Bashan; his appetite will be satisfied on the hills of Ephraim and Gilead.

Jeremiah 50:33,34 This is what the Lord Almighty says: "The people of Israel are oppressed, and the people of Judah as well. All their captors hold them fast, refusing to let them go. Yet their redeemer is strong; the Lord Almighty is his name. He will vigorously defend their cause so that he may bring rest to their land, but unrest to those who live in Babylon."

Jeremiah 51:5,6 For Israel and Judah have not been forsaken by their God, the Lord Almighty, though their land is full of guilt before the Holy One of Israel. Flee from Babylon! Run for your lives! Do not be destroyed because of her sins. It is time for the Lord's vengenance, he will pay her what she deserves.

Jeremiah 51:33 This is what the Lord Almighty, the God of Israel, says: "The Daughter of Babylon is like a threshing floor at the time it is trampled; the time to harvest her will soon come."

Jeremiah 51:45   Come out of her, my people! Run for your lives! Run from the fierce anger of the Lord.

Jeremiah 51:50   You who have escaped the sword, leave and do not linger! Remember the Lord in a distant land, and think on Jerusalem.

Lamentations 4:22a   O Daughter of Zion your punishment will end; he will not prolong your exile.

Ezekiel 11:16,17   Therefore say: "This is what the Sovereign Lord says: Although I sent them far away among the nations and scattered them among the countries, yet for a little while I have been a sanctuary for them in the countries where they have gone." Therefore say: "This is what the Sovereign Lord says: I will gather you from the nations and bring you back from the countries where you have been scattered, and I will give you back the land of Israel again."

Ezekiel 20:34-38   I will bring you from the nations and gather you from the countries where you have been scattered — with a mighty hand and an outstretched arm and with outpoured wrath. I will bring you into the desert of the nations and there, face to face, I will execute judgment upon you. As I judged your fathers in the desert of the land of Egypt, so I will judge you, declares the Sovereign Lord. I will take note of you as you pass under my staff, and I will bring you into the bond of the covenant. I will purge you of those who revolt and rebel against me. Although I will bring them out of the land where they are living, yet they will not enter the land of Israel. Then you will know that I am the Lord.

Ezekiel 20:41,42   I will accept you as fragrant incense when I bring you out from the nations and gather you from the countries where you have been scattered, and I will show myself holy among you in the sight of the nations. Then you will know that I am the Lord, when I bring you into the land of Israel, the land I had sworn with uplifted hand to give to your fathers.

Ezekiel 28:25   This is what the Sovereign Lord says: When I gather the people of Israel from the nations where they have been scattered, I will show myself holy among them in the sight of the nations. Then they will live in their own land, which I gave to my servant Jacob.

Ezekiel 34:13   I will bring them out from the nations and gather them from the countries, and I will bring them into their own land.

Ezekiel 36 "Son of man, prophesy to the mountains of Israel and say, 'O mountains of Israel, hear the word of the Lord. This is what the Sovereign Lord says: The enemy said of you "Aha! The ancient heights have become our posession." ' Therefore prophesy and say, 'This is what the Sovereign Lord says: Because they ravaged and hounded you from every side so that you became the possession of the rest of the nations and the object of people's malicious talk and slander, therefore, O mountains of Israel, hear the word of the Sovereign Lord: This is what the Sovereign Lord says to the mountains and hills, to the ravines and valleys, to the desolate ruins and the deserted towns that have been plundered and ridiculed by the rest of the nations around you — this is what the Sovereign Lord says: In my burning zeal I have spoken against the rest of the nations, and against all Edom, for with glee and with malice in their hearts they made my land their own posession so that they might plunder its pastureland.' Therefore prophesy concerning the land of Israel and say to the mountains and hills, to the ravines and valleys: 'This is what the Sovereign Lord says: I speak in my jealous wrath because you have suffered the scorn of the nations. Therefore this is what the Sovereign Lord says: I swear with uplifted hand that the nations around you will also suffer scorn. 'But you, O mountains of Israel, will produce branches and fruit for my people Israel, for they will soon come home. I am concerned for you and will look on you with favor; you will be plowed and sown, and I will multiply the number of people upon you, even the whole house of Israel. The towns will be inhabited and the ruins rebuilt. I will increase the number of men and animals upon you, and they will be fruitful and become numerous. I will settle people on you as in the past and will make you prosper more than before. Then you will know that I am the Lord. I will cause people, my people Israel, to walk upon you. They will possess you, and you will be their inheritance; you will never again deprive them of their children. This is what the Sovereign Lord says: Because people say to you, "You devour men and deprive your nation of its children," therefore you will no longer devour men or make your nation childless, declares the Sovereign Lord. No longer will I make you hear the taunts of the nations, and no longer will you suffer the scorn of the peoples or cause your nation to fall, declares the Sovereign Lord.' " Again the word of the Lord came to me: "Son of man, when the people of Israel were living in their own land, they defiled it by their conduct and their actions. Their conduct was like a woman's monthly uncleanness in my sight. So I poured out my wrath on them because they had shed blood in the land and because they had defiled it with their idols. I dispersed them among the nations and they were scattered through the countries; I judged them according to their conduct and their actions. And wherever they went among the nations they profaned my holy name, for it was said of them, 'These are the Lord's people, and yet they had to leave his land.' I had concern for my holy name, which the house of Israel profaned among the nations where they had gone. "Therefore say to the house of Israel, 'This is what the Sovereign Lord says: It is not for your sake, O house of Israel, that I am going to do these things, but for the sake of my holy name, which you have profaned among the nations where you have gone. I will show the holiness of my great name, which has been profaned among the nations, the name you have profaned among them. Then the nations will know that I am the Lord, declares the Sovereign Lord, when I show myself holy through you before their eyes. 'For I will take you out of the nations; I will gather you from all the countries and bring you back into your own land. I will sprinkle clean water on you, and you will be clean; I will cleanse you from all your impurities and from all your idols. I will give you a new heart and put a new spirit in you; I will remove from you your heart of stone and give you a heart of flesh. And I will put my Spirit in you and move you to follow my decrees and be careful to keep my laws. You will live in the land I gave your forefathers; you will be my people, and I will be your God. I will save you from all your uncleanness. I will call for the grain and make it plentiful and will not bring famine upon you. I will increase the fruit of the trees and the crops of the field, so that you will no longer suffer disgrace among the nations because of famine. Then you will remember your evil ways and wicked deeds, and you will loathe yourselves for your sins and detestable practices. I want you to know that I am not doing this for your sake, declares the Sovereign Lord. Be ashamed and disgraced for your conduct, O house of Israel! This is what the Sovereign Lord says: On the day I cleanse you from all your sins, I will resettle your towns, and the ruins will be rebuilt. The desolate land will be cultivated instead of lying desolate in the sight of all who pass through it. They will say, "This land that was laid waste has become like the garden of Eden; the cities that were lying in ruins, desolate and destroyed, are now fortified and inhabited." Then the nations around you that remain will know that I the Lord have rebuilt what was destroyed and have replanted what was desolate. I the Lord have spoken and I will do it." "This is what the Sovereign Lord says: Once again I will yield to the plea of the house of Israel and do this for them: I will make their people as numerous as sheep, as numerous as the flocks for offerings at Jerusalem during her appointed feasts. So will the ruined cities be filled with flocks of people. Then they will know that I am the Lord."

Ezekiel 37 The hand of the Lord was upon me, and he brought me out by the Spirit of the Lord and set me in the middle of a valley; it was full of bones. He led me back and forth among them, and I saw a great many bones on the floor of the valley, bones that were very dry. He asked me, "Son of man, can these bones live?" I said, "O Sovereign Lord, you alone know." Then he said to me, "Prophesy to these bones and say to them, 'Dry bones, hear the word of the Lord! This is what the Sovereign Lord says to these bones: I will make breath enter you, and you will come to life. I will attach tendrons to you and make flesh come upon you and cover you with skin; I will put breath in you, and you will come to life. Then you will know that I am the Lord.' " So I prophesied as I was commanded. And as I was prophesying, there was a noise, a rattling sound, and the bones came together, bone to bone. I looked, and tendons and flesh appeared on them and skin covered them, but there was no breath in them. Then he said to me, "Prophesy to the breath; prophesy, son of man, and say to it, 'This is what the Sovereign Lord says: Come from the four winds, O breath, and breathe into these slain, that they may live.' " So I prophesied as he commanded me, and breathe entered them; they came to life and stood up on their feet — a vast army. Then he said to me: "Son of man, these bones are the whole house of Israel. They say, 'Our bones are dried up and our hope is gone; we are cut off. Therefore prophesy and say to them: 'This is what the Sovereign Lord says: O my people, I am going to open your graves and bring you up from them; I will bring you back to the land of Israel. Then you, my people, will know that I am the Lord, when I open your graves and bring you up from them. I will put my Spirit in you and you will live, and I will settle you in your own land. Then you will know that I the Lord have spoken, and I have done it, declares the Lord.' " The word of the Lord came to me: "Son of man, take a stick of wood and write on it, 'Belonging to Judah and the Israelites associated with him.' Then take another stick of wood, and write on it, 'Ephraim's stick, belonging to Joseph and all the house of Israel associated with him.' Join them together into one stick so that they will become one in your hand. "When your countrymen ask you, 'Won't you tell us what you mean by this?' say to them, 'This is what the Sovereign Lord says: I am going to take the stick of Joseph — which is in Ephraim's hand — and of the Israelite tribes associated with him, and join it to Judah's stick, making them a single stick of wood, and they will become one in my hand.' Hold before their eyes the sticks you have written on and say to them, 'This is what the Sovereign Lord says: I will take the Israelites out of the nations where they have gone. I will gather them from all around and bring them back into their own land. I will make them one nation in the land, on the mountains of Israel. There will be one king over all of them and they will never again be two nations or be divided into two kingdoms. They will no longer defile themselves with their idols and vile images or with any of their offenses, for I will save them from all their sinful backsliding, and I will cleanse them. They will be my people, and I will be their God. 'My servant David will be king over them, and they will all have **one shepherd**. They will follow my laws and be careful to keep my decrees. They will live in the land I gave to my servant Jacob, the land where your fathers lived. They and their children and their children's children will live there forever, and David my servant will be their prince forever. I will make a covenant of peace with them; it will be an everlasting covenant. I will establish them and increase their numbers, and I will put my sanctuary among them forever. My dwelling place will be with them; I will be their God, and they will be my people. Then the nations will know that I the Lord make Israel holy, when my sanctuary is among them forever.' "

Ezekiel 37:21,22 This is what the Sovereign Lord says: "I will take the Israelites out of the nations where they have gone. I will gather them from all around and bring them back into their own land. I will make them one nation in the land, on the mountains of Israel. There will be one king over all of them and they will never again be two nations or be divided into two kingdoms."

Ezekiel 38:8 (of Gog) . . . After many days you will be called to arms. In future years you will invade a land that has recovered from war, whose people were gathered from many nations to the mountains of Israel, which had long been desolate. They had been brought out from the nations, and now all of them live in safety.

Ezekiel 39:25-29 Therefore this is what the Sovereign Lord says: "I will now bring Jacob back from captivity; and will have compassion on all the people of Israel, and I will be zealous for my holy name. They will forget their shame and all the unfaithfulness they showed toward me when they lived in safety in their land with no one to make them afraid. When I have brought them back from the nations and have gathered them from the countries of their enemies, I will show myself holy through them in the sight of many nations. Then they will know that I am the Lord their God, for though I sent them into exile among the nations, I will gather them to their own land, not leaving any behind. I will no longer hide my face from them, for I will pour out my Spirit on the house of Israel, declares the Sovereign Lord."

Ezekiel 45-48   Division of the Land, Offerings and Holy Days, Boundaries, gates of the city.

Ezekiel 47:13,14   This is what the Sovereign Lord says: "These are the boundaries by which you are to divide the land for an inheritance among the twelve tribes of Israel, with two portions for Joseph. You are to divide it equally among them. Because I swore with uplifted hand to give it to your forefathers, this land will become your inheritance.

Daniel 12   (Deliverance of the Jewish people in the last days) At that time Michael (the Archangel), the great prince who protects your people will arise.

Hosea 1:10,11   Yet the Israelites will be the sand on the seashore, which cannot be measured or counted. In the place where it was said to them, "You are not my people," they will be called "sons of the living God." The people of Judah and the people of Israel will be reunited, and they will appoint one leader and will come up out of the land, for great will be the day of Jezrell.

Hosea 3:4,5   For the Israelites will live many days without king or prince, without sacrifice or sacred stones, without ephod or idol. Afterward the Israelites will return and seek the Lord their God and David their king. They will come trembling to the Lord and to his blessings in the last days.

Hosea 6:11   Also for you, Judah, a harvest is appointed. Whenever I would restore the fortunes of my people.

Hosea 8:10   Although they have sold themslves among the nations, I will now gather them together.

Hosea 11:1   When Israel was a child, I loved him, and out of Egypt I called my son.

Hosea 14:1   Return, O Israel, to the Lord your God.

Hosea 14:7   Men will dwell again in his shade. He will flourish like the grain. He will blossom like a vine, and his fame will be like the wine from Lebanon.

Joel 2:18,19 Then the Lord will be jealous for his land and take pity on his people. The Lord will reply to them: "I am sending you grain, new wine and oil, enough to satisfy you fully; never again will I make you an object of scorn to the nations."

Joel 2:32 And everyone who calls on the name of the Lord will be saved; for on Mount Zion and in Jerusalem there will be deliverance, as the Lord has said, among the survivors whom the Lord calls.

Joel 3:1,2 In those days and at that time, when I restore the fortunes of Judah and Jerusalem I will gather all nations and bring them down to the Valley of Jehoshaphat. There I will enter into judgment against them concerning my inheritance, my people Israel, for they scattered my people among the nations and divided up my land.

Joel 3:14-16 Multitudes, multitudes in the valley of decision! For the day of the Lord is near in the valley of decision. The sun and moon will be darkened, and the stars no longer shine. The Lord will roar from Zion and thunder from Jerusalem; the earth and the sky will tremble, But the Lord will be a refuge for his people, a stronghold for the people of Israel.

Joel 3:20 Judah will be inhabited forever and Jerusalem through all generations.

Amos 2:10 I brought you up out of Egypt, and I led you forty years in the desert to give you the land of the Amorites.

Amos 5:4 This is what the Lord says to the house of Israel: "Seek me and live."

Amos 9:14,15 "I will bring back my exiled people Israel; they will rebuild the ruined cities and live in them. They will plant vineyards and drink their wine; they will make gardens and eat their fruit. I will plant Israel in their own land never again to be uprooted from the land I have given them," says the Lord your God.

Obadiah 1:17,19 "But on Mount Zion will be deliverance; it will be holy, and the house of Jacob will possess its inheritance. People from the Negev will occupy the mountains of Esau, and people from the foothills will possess the land of the Philistines. They will occupy the fields of Ephraim and Samaria, and Benjamin will possess Gilead.

Obadiah 1:20,21 This company of Israelite exiles who are in Canaan will possess the land as far as Zarephath; the exiles from Jerusalem who are in Sepharad will possess the towns of the Negev. Deliverers will go up on Mount Zion to govern the mountains of Esau. And the kingdom will be the Lord's.

Jonah 2:8 Those who cling to worthless idols forfeit the grace that could be theirs.

Micah 2;12,13 I will surely gather all of you, O Jacob; I will surely bring together the remnant of Israel. I will bring them together like sheep in a pen, like a flock in its pasture; the place will throng with people. One who *breaks open the way* will go up before them; they will break through the gate and go out. Their king will pass through before them, the Lord at their head.

Micah 4:1,2 In the last days the mountain of the Lord's temple will be established as chief among the mountains; it will be raised above the hills, and peoples will stream to it. Many nations will come and say, "Come, let us go up to the mountain of the Lord, to the house of the God of Jacob. He will teach us his ways, so that we may walk in his paths." The law will go out from Zion, the word of the Lord from Jerusalem.

Micah 4:6,7 "In that day," declares the Lord, "I will gather the lame; I will assemble the exiles and those driven away a strong nation. The Lord will rule over them in Mount Zion from that day and forever."

Micah 4:10-13 Writhe in agony, O Daughter of Zion, like a woman in labor, for now you must leave the city to camp in the open field. You will go to Babylon; there you will be rescued. There the Lord will redeem you out of the hand of your enemies. But now many nations are gathered against you. They say, "Let her be defiled, let our eyes gloat over Zion!" But they do not know the thoughts of the Lord; they do not understand his plan, he who gathers them like sheaves to the threshing floor. "Rise and thresh, O Daughter of Zion, for I will give you horns of iron; I will give you hoofs of bronze and you will break to pieces many nations." You will devote their ill-gotten gains to the Lord, their wealth to the Lord of all the earth.

Micah 5:2-4 But you, Bethlehem Ephrathan, though you are small among the clans of Judah, out of you will come for me one who will be ruler over Israel, whose origins are from of old, from ancient times. Therefore Israel will be abandoned until the time when she who is in labor gives birth and the rest of his brothers return to join the Israelites.

Micah 7:14,15 Shepherd your people with your staff, the flock of your inheritance, which lives by itself in a forest, in fertile pasturelands. Let them feed in Bashan and Gilead as in days long ago. "As in the days when you came out of Egypt, I will show them my wonders."

Micah 7:18-20   Who is a God like you, who pardons sin and forgives the transgression of the remnant of his inheritance? You do not stay angry forever but delight to show mercy. You will again have compassion on us; you will tread our sins underfoot and hurl all our iniquities into the depths of the sea. You will be true to Jacob, and show mercy to Abraham, as you pledged on oath to our fathers in days long ago.

Nahum 1:15   Look, there on the mountains, the feet of one who brings good news, who proclaims peace. Celebrate your festivals, O Judah, and fulfill your vows. No more will the wicked invade you; they will be completely destroyed.

Zephaniah 2:1,2   Gather together, gather together, O shameful nation, before the appointed time arrives and that day sweeps on like chaff, before the fierce anger of the Lord comes upon you, before the day of the Lord's wrath comes upon you.

Zephaniah 2:9   "Therefore, as surely as I live," declares the Lord Almighty, the God of Israel, "surely Moab will become like Sodom, the Ammonites like Gomorrah — a place of weeds and salt pits, a wasteland forever. The remnant of my people will plunder them; the survivors of my nation will inherit their land."

Zephaniah 3:8   "Therefore wait for me," declares the Lord, "for the day I will stand up to testify. I have decided to assemble the nations, to gather the kingdoms and to pour out my wrath on them — all my fierce anger. The whole world will be consumed by the fire of my jealous anger."

Zephaniah 3:19,20   At that time I will deal with all who opposed you; I will rescue the lame and gather those who have been scattered. I will give them praise and honor in every land where they were put to shame. "At that time I will gather you: at that time I will bring you home. I will give you honor and praise among all the peoples of the earth when I restore your fortunes before your very eyes," says the Lord.

Haggai 2:6-9   This is what the Lord Almighty says: "In a little while I will once more shake the heavens and the earth, the sea and the dry land. I will shake all nations, and the desired of all nations will come, and I will fill this house with glory," says the Lord Almighty. "The silver is mine and the gold is mine," declares the Lord Almighty. "The glory of this present house will be greater than the glory of the former house," says the Lord Almighty. "And in this place I will grant peace," declares the Lord Almighty.

Zechariah 2:6,7 "Come! Come! Flee from the land of the north," declares the Lord, "for I have scattered you to the four winds of heaven" declares the Lord. "Come, O Zion! Escape, you who live in the Daughter of Babylon!"

Zechariah 2:10-13 "Shout and be glad, O Daughter of Zion. For I am coming, and I will live among you," declares the Lord. "Many nations will be joined with the Lord in that day and will become my people. I will live among you and you will know that the Lord Almighty has sent me to you. The Lord will inherit Judah as his portion in the holy land and will again choose Jerusalem. Be still before the Lord, all mankind, because he has roused himself from his holy dwelling."

Zechariah 8:7,8 This is what the Lord Almighty says: "I will save my people from the countries of the east and the west. I will bring them back to live in Jerusalem; They will be my people, and I will be faithful and righteous to them as their God."

Zechariah 8:13 As you have been an object of cursing among the nations, O Judah and Israel, so will I save you, and you will be a blessing. Do not be afraid, but let your hands be stong.

Zechariah 8:20-23 This is what the Lord Almighty says: "Many peoples and the inhabitants of many cities will yet come, and the inhabitants of one city will go to another and say, 'Let us go at once to entreat the Lord and seek the Lord Almighty. I myself am going.' And many peoples and powerful nations will come to Jerusalem to seek the Lord Almighty and to entreat him." This is what the Lord Almighty says: "In those days ten men from all languages and nations will take firm hold of one Jew by the edge of his robe and say, 'Let us go with you, because we have heard that God is with you.' "

Zechariah 9:16 The Lord their God will save them on that day as the flock of his people. They will sparkle in his land like jewels in a crown.

Zechariah 10:6 I will strengthen the house of Judah and save the house of Joseph. I will restore them because I have compassion on them. They will be as though I had not rejected them, for I am the Lord their God and I will answer them.

Zechariah 10:8-10   I will signal for them and gather them in. Surely I will redeem them; they will be as numerous as before. Though I scatter them among the peoples, yet in distant lands they will remember me. They and their children will survive, and they will return. I will bring them back from Egypt and gather them from Assyria. I will bring them to Gilead and Lebanon, and there will not be room enough for them.

Zechariah 13:8,9   "In the whole land," declares the Lord, "two-thirds will be struck down and perish; yet one-third will be left in it. This third I will bring into the fire; I will refine them like silver and test them like gold. They will call on my name and I will answer them; I will say, 'They are my people,' and they will say, 'The Lord is our God.' "

Zechariah 14:14   Judah too will fight at Jerusalem. The wealth of all the surrounding nations will be collected — great quantities of gold and silver and clothing.

Zechariah 14:16   Then the survivors from all the nations that have attacked Jerusalem will go up year after year to worship the King, the Lord Almighty, and to celebrate the Feast of Tabernacles.

Appendix B
ZIONIST DOCUMENTS
The Basel Program

The basic document of the Jewish national revival, this was formulated at the First Zionist Congress, which took place in Basel, Switzerland in August 1897, and was accepted as the policy of the movement until the establishment of an independent State of Israel in 1948.

Zionism strives to create for the Jewish people a home in Palestine secured by public law.

The Congress contemplates the following means to the attainment of this end:

1. The promotion, on suitable lines, of the colonization of Palestine by Jewish agricultural and industrial workers.

2. The organization and binding together of the whole of Jewry by means of appropriate institutions, local and international, in accordance with the laws of each country.

3. The strengthening and fostering of Jewish national sentiment and consciousness.

4. Preparatory steps towards obtaining Government consent, where necessary, to the attainment of the aim of Zionism.

"In Basel I Founded the Jewish State"

An extract from Theodore Herzl's diary for September 3, 1897. He had just returned to Vienna after the Congress, and this is how he assessed its achievements.

Were I to sum up the Basel Congress in a word — which I shall guard against pronouncing publicly — it would be this: At Basel I founded the Jewish State.

If I said this out loud today I would be answered by universal laughter. Perhaps in five years, and certainly in fifty, everyone will know it. The foundation of a State lies in the will of the people for a State, yes, even in the will of one sufficiently powerful individual (*l'Etat c'est moi* — Louis XIV). Territory is only the material basis; the State, even when it possesses territory, is always something abstract. The Church State exists even without it; otherwise the Pope would not be sovereign.

At Basel, then, I created this abstraction which, as such, is invisible to the vast majority of people. And with infinitesimal means, I gradually worked the people into the mood for a State and made them feel that they were its National Assembly.

The Balfour Declaration

Britain's wartime statement of sympathy with Zionism. There were many drafts, and the final version is a careful compromise that eschewed an exact definition of what was intended by the term "National Home" and was at the root of much subsequent controversy.

Foreign Office,
November 2nd, 1917

Dear Lord Rothschild,

I have much pleasure in conveying to you, on behalf of His Majesty's Government, the following declaration of sympathy with Jewish Zionist aspirations which has been submitted to, and approved by, the Cabinet.

His Majesty's Government view with favour the establishment in Palestine of a national home for the Jewish people, and will use their best endeavours to facilitate the achievement of this object, it being clearly understood that nothing shall be done which may prejudice the civil and religious rights of existing non-Jewish communities in Palestine, or the rights and political status enjoyed by Jews in any other country.

I should be grateful if you would bring this declaration to the knowledge of the Zionist Federation.

Yours sincerely,
Arthur James Balfour

The Proclamation of Independence

This was read by David Ben-Gurion on May 14, 1948, in a small building then being used as the town museum in Tel Aviv, before a small gathering. Signatories to the Declaration were the thirty-seven members of the Provisional State Council.

The Land of Israel was the birthplace of the Jewish people. Here their spiritual, religious and national identity was formed. Here they achieved independence and created a culture of national and universal significance. Here they wrote and gave the Bible to the world.

Exiled from the Land of Israel, the Jewish people remained faithful to it in all the countries of their dispersion, never ceasing to pray and hope for their return and the restoration of their national freedom.

Impelled by this historic association Jews strove throughout the centuries to go back to the land of their fathers and regain their statehood. In recent decades they returned in their masses. They reclaimed the wilderness, revived their language, built cities and villages, and established a vigorous and ever-growing community, with its own economic and cultural life. They sought peace yet were prepared to defend themselves. They brought the blessings of progress to all inhabitants of the country and looked forward to sovereign independence.

In the year 1897 the First Zionist Congress, inspired by Theodore Herzl's vision of the Jewish State, proclaimed the right of the Jewish people to national revival in their own country.

This right was acknowledged by the Balfour Declaration of November 2, 1917, and re-affirmed by the Mandate of the League of Nations, which gave explicit international recognition to the historic connection of the Jewish people with Palestine and their right to reconstitute their National Home.

The recent holocaust, which engulfed millions of Jews in Europe, proved anew the need to solve the problem of the homelessness and lack of independence of the Jewish people by means of the re-establishment of the Jewish State, which would open the gates to all Jews and endow the Jewish people with equality of status among the family of nations.

The survivors of the disastrous slaughter in Europe, and also

Jews from other lands, have not desisted from their efforts to reach Eretz-Israel, in face of difficulties, obstacles and perils; and have not ceased to urge their right to a life of dignity, freedom and honest toil in the their ancestral land.

In the Second World War the Jewish people in Palestine made their full contribution to the struggle of the freedom-loving nations against the Nazi evil. The sacrifices of their soldiers and their war effort gained them the right to rank with the nations which founded the United Nations.

On November 29, 1947, the General Assembly of the United Nations adopted a Resolution requiring the establishment of a Jewish State in Palestine. The General Assembly called upon the inhabitants of the country to take all the necessary steps on their part to put the plan into effect. This recognition by the United Nations of the right of the Jewish people to establish their independent State is unassailable.

It is the natural right of the Jewish people to lead, as do all other nations, an independent existence in its sovereign State.

ACCORDINGLY WE, the members of the National Council, representing the Jewish people in Palestine, and the World Zionist Movement, are met together in solemn assembly today, the day of termination of the British Mandate for Palestine; and by virtue of the natural and historic right of the Jewish people and of the Resolution of the General Assembly of the United Nations.

WE HEREBY PROCLAIM the establishment of the Jewish State in Palestine, to be called "Medinat Israel" (The State of Israel).

WE HEREBY DECLARE that, as from the termination of the Mandate at midnight, the 14th-15th May, 1948, and pending the setting up of the duly elected bodies of the State in accordance with a Constitution, to be drawn up by the Constituent Assembly not later than the 1st October, 1948, the National Council shall act as the Provisional State Council, and that the National Administration shall constitute the Provisional Government of the Jewish State, which shall be known as Israel.

THE STATE OF ISRAEL will be open to the immigration of Jews from all countries of their dispersion; will promote the development of the country for the benefit of all its inhabitants;

will be based on the principles of liberty, justice and peace as conceived by the prophets of Israel, will uphold the full social and political equality of all its citizens, without distinction of religion, race or sex; will guarantee freedom of religion, conscience, education and culture; will safeguard the Holy Places of all religions; and will loyally uphold the principles of the United Nations Charter.

THE STATE OF ISRAEL will be ready to cooperate with the organs and representatives of the United Nations in the implementation of the Resolution of the Assembly of November 29, 1947, and will take steps to bring about the Economic Union over the whole of Palestine.

We appeal to the United Nations to assist the Jewish people in the building of its State and to admit Israel into the family of nations.

In the midst of wanton aggression, we yet call upon the Arab inhabitants of the State of Israel to preserve the ways of peace and play their part in the development of the State, on the basis of full and equal citizenship and due representation in all its bodies and institutions — provisional and permanent.

We extend our hand in peace and neighborliness to all the neighboring states and their peoples, and invite them to cooperate with the independent Jewish nation for the common good of all. The State of Israel is prepared to make its contribution to the progress of the Middle East as a whole.

Our call goes out to the Jewish people all over the world to rally to our side in the task of immigration and development and to stand by us in the great struggle for the fulfilment of the dream of generations for the redemption of Israel.

With trust in Almighty God, we set our hand to this Declaration, at this Session of the Provisional State Council, on the soil of the Homeland, in the city of Tel Aviv, on this Sabbath eve, the fifth of Iyar, 5708, the fourteenth day of May, 1948.

(The signatories) David Ben-Gurion, Daniel Auster, Mordechai Bentov, Isaac Ben-Zvi, Eliyahu Berligne, Fritz (Peretz) Bernstein, Rabbi Wolf Gold, Meir Grabovsky, Isaac Gruenbaum, Dr. Abraham Granovsky (Granott), Eliyahu Dobkin, Meir Wilner-Kovner, Zerach Wahrhaftig, Herzl Vardi, Rachel Cohen, Rabbi Kalman Kahana,

Saadia Kobashi, Rabbi Isaac Meir Levin, Meir David Loewenstein, Zvi Luria, Golda Myerson (Meir), Nachum Nir, Zvi Segal, Rabbi Yehuda Leib Fishman (Maimon), David Zvi Pinkas, Aharon Zisling, Moshe Kolodny (Kol), Eliezer Kaplan, Abraham Katznelson, Felix Rosenblueth (Rosen), David Remez, Berl Repetur, Mordechai Shattner, Ben Zion Sternberg, Bechor Shitreet, Moshe Shapira, Moshe Shertok (Sharett).

Appendix C

Jewish Population Statistics

To help you pray for, warn and otherwise help the Jewish people return to Israel.

Used by permission of the American Jewish Yearbook 1987

RANK-ORDERED METROPOLITAN STATISTICAL AREAS, 1986, BY JEWISH POPULATION

Metro Area	Estimated Jewish Population	Jewish % of Total Population	% Share of U.S. Jewish Population	Cumulative % Share of Jewish Population
1. New York-Northern N.J.*	2,216,000	12.4	38.1	38.1
2. Los Angeles*	604,000	4.7	10.4	48.5
3. Miami-Ft. Lauderdale*	367,000	12.8	6.3	54.8
4. Philadelphia-Wilmington-Trenton*	309,000	5.4	5.3	60.1
5. Chicago*	254,000	3.1	4.4	64.5
6. Boston*	235,000	5.8	4.0	68.6
7. Washington, D.C.	159,000	4.6	2.7	71.3
8. San Francisco-Oakland-San Jose*	136,000	2.3	2.3	73.6
9. Baltimore	101,000	4.5	1.7	75.3
10. W. Palm Beach-Boca Raton	95,000	13.1	1.6	77.0
11. Cleveland-Akron*	77,000	2.8	1.3	78.3
12. Detroit-Ann Arbor*	74,000	1.6	1.3	79.6
13. St. Louis	54,000	2.2	0.9	80.5
14. Atlanta	52,000	2.1	.9	81.4
15. Pittsburgh*	47,000	2.0	.8	82.2
16. Phoenix	45,000	2.4	.8	83.0
17. Denver-Boulder*	45,000	2.5	.8	83.7
18. Houston-Galveston*	43,000	1.2	.7	84.5

TABLE 4B.—*(Continued)*

Metro Area	Estimated Jewish Population	Jewish % of Total Population	% Share of U.S. Jewish Population	Cumulative % Share of Jewish Population
19. San Diego	37,000	1.2	.6	85.1
20. Minneapolis-St. Paul	30,000	1.3	.5	85.6
21. Hartford	28,000	2.7	.5	86.1
22. Dallas-Ft. Worth*	27,000	0.8	.5	86.6
23. Milwaukee*	24,000	1.6	.4	87.0
24. New Haven	24,000	4.7	.4	87.4
25. Cincinnati*	23,000	1.4	.4	87.8
26. Kansas City	22,000	1.5	.4	88.2
27. Seattle-Tacoma*	20,000	0.9	.3	88.6
28. Rochester	20,000	2.1	.3	88.9
29. Tampa-St. Petersburg	20,000	1.1	.3	89.2
30. Albany-Schenectady-Troy	20,000	2.3	.3	89.5

Sources: Boundaries and general population estimates, Bureau of the Census, June 1985. Areas marked * = CMSA (Consolidated Metropolitan Statistical Area); otherwise unit is PMSA (Primary Metropolitan Statistical Area). Jewish figures, Appendix table A-3, below.

1986 JEWISH POPULATION ESTIMATES

The Jewish population of the United States in 1986 was estimated to be 5.814 million. This figure is approximately the same order of magnitude as that reported for 1985.

The basic population units used in this analysis are the fund-raising areas of local Jewish federations. These geographic units vary in size and may represent several towns, one county, or an aggregate of several counties. Some estimates, from areas without federations, are from UJA field representatives. Still other estimates have been given by local rabbis and other informed Jewish community leaders.

TABLE A-3. COMMUNITIES WITH JEWISH POPULATIONS OF 100 OR MORE, 1986 (ESTIMATED)

State and City	Jewish Population
ALABAMA	
Anniston	100
*Auburn	100
*Birmingham	5,100
Dothan	205
Florence (incl. in Sheffield total)	
Gadsden	180
Huntsville	550
Jasper	130
**Mobile	1,250
**Montgomery	1,650
Selma	210
Sheffield	150
Tuscaloosa	315
Tuscumbia (incl. in Sheffield total)	
ALASKA	
Anchorage	600
Fairbanks	210
ARIZONA	
*Flagstaff	250
*Phoenix	45,000
*Tucson	18,000
Yuma	100
ARKANSAS	
Fayetteville	120
Ft. Smith	160
Helena	100
Hot Springs (incl. in Little Rock)	
**Little Rock	1,250
Pine Bluff	100
Southeast Arkansas[N]	140
***Wynne-Forest City	110

State and City	Jewish Population
CALIFORNIA	
Alameda & Contra Costa counties	35,000
Antelope Valley	375
Bakersfield (incl. in Kern County)	
Berkeley (incl. in Alameda & Contra Costa total)	
***El Centro	125
***Elsinore	250
Eureka	250
***Fontana	165
*Fresno	2,000
Kern County	850
Lancaster (incl. in Antelope Valley)	
Long Beach (also incl. in Los Angeles total)[N]	13,500
Los Angeles Metro. Area	500,870
***Merced	100
Modesto	260
Monterey	1,500
Oakland (incl. in Alameda & Contra Costa counties)	
Ontario (incl. in Pomona Valley)	
Orange County	80,000
Palm Springs[N]	8,950
Pasadena (also incl. in L.A. Metro. Area)	2,000
Petaluma	800
Pomona Valley[N]	3,500
Riverside	1,325
Sacramento[N]	10,000
Salinas	350

State and City	Jewish Population
San Bernardino	2,065
*San Diego	37,000
San Francisco[N]	80,000
*San Jose (Palo Alto & Los Altos incl. in San Francisco total)	18,000
San Luis Obispo	450
***San Pedro	300
*Santa Barbara	3,800
Santa Cruz	1,000
Santa Maria	200
Santa Monica (also incl. in Los Angeles total)	8,000
Santa Rosa	750
*Stockton	1,500
***Sun City	800
Tulare & Kings County	500
Vallejo	400
*Ventura County	7,000
COLORADO	
Boulder (incl. in Denver total)	
Colorado Springs	1,000
Denver[N]	45,000
*Ft. Collins	1,000
Greely	100
Loveland (incl. in Ft. Collins total)	
Pueblo	375
CONNECTICUT	
Bridgeport[N]	18,000
Bristol	250
Colchester	525
Danbury[N]	3,500
Greenwich	4,950
Hartford[N]	26,000

| | Jewish | | Jewish | | Jewish |
State and City	Population	State and City	Population	State and City	Population

***Lebanon........ 175
Lower Middlesex
County (incl. in New
London)
Manchester (incl. in
Hartford)
Meriden........ 1,400
Middletown..... 1,300
***Moodus........ 150
New Haven^N... 22,000
New London^N... 3,600
***New Milford.... 200
Newtown (incl. in
Danbury)
Norwalk^N 4,000
Norwich........ 2,500
Putnam 110
Rockville (incl. in
Hartford)
Shelton (incl. in Valley
Area)
Stamford/New Canaan
.... 12,000
Torrington........ 560
Valley Area^N...... 700
***Wallingford..... 440
Waterbury^N..... 2,700
Westport (also incl. in
Norwalk)...... 2,800
Willimantic 400
***Winsted 110

DELAWARE
Wilmington (incl.rest of
state) 9,500

DISTRICT OF COLUMBIA
Greater Washington^N
.... 157,335

FLORIDA
Boca Raton-Delray
.... 45,000
Brevard County . 2,250

**Daytona Beach . 2,000
Fort Lauderdale^{N}60,000
Fort Pierce 270
Gainesville...... 1,000
Hollywood^N ... 60,000
**Jacksonville.... 6,800
Key West......... 170
Lakeland 800
Lee County (incl. Ft.
Myers)........ 3,500
Lehigh Acres...... 125
*Miami (incl.all of Dade
County).... 247,000
**Orlando 9,000
Palm Beach County
(excl. Boca Raton-Del-
ray) 50,000
Pensacola........ 400
Port Charlotte..... 150
**Sarasota 8,500
***St. Augustine.... 100
*St.Petersburg (incl.
Clearwater).... 9,500
Tallahassee 1,000
*Tampa 10,500

GEORGIA
Albany........... 525
Athens........... 250
Atlanta Metro. Area
.... 52,000
Augusta^N....... 1,400
***Brunswick 120
**Columbus 1,000
Dalton 235
Fitzgerald-Cordele . 125
Macon 900
*Savannah 2,600
Valdosta......... 145

HAWAII
Hilo 280
Honolulu (incl. all of
Oahu) 7,000

Kuaii 100
Maui 220

IDAHO
Boise 120
Lewiston 100
Moscow (incl. in Lewis-
ton total)

ILLINOIS
Aurora........... 320
Bloomington 125
*Champaign-Urbana
.... 2,000
Chicago Metro. Area
.... 248,000
Danville.......... 240
*Decatur 230
East St. Louis (incl. in
Southern Ill.)
Elgin^N 700
Galesburg 120
*Joliet 850
Kankakee......... 260
*Peoria.......... 1,200
Quad Cities^N.... 1,700
Quincy........... 200
Rock Island (incl. in
Quad Cities)
Rockford^N........ 975
Southern Illinois^N.. 900
*Springfield 1,100
***Sterling-Dixon... 110
Waukegan 1,200

INDIANA
Anderson......... 105
Bloomington 300
Elkart (incl. in South
Bend)
***Evansville 1,200
Ft. Wayne...... 1,170
Gary (incl. in Northwest
Ind.-Calumet Region)

State and City	Jewish Population	State and City	Jewish Population	State and City	Jewish Population
**Indianapolis...	10,000	LOUISIANA		MASSACHUSETTS	
Lafayette[N]	600	***Alexandria	700	Amherst	750
Marion	170	Baton Rouge[N]	1,400	Andover[N]	3,000
*Michigan City	430	Lafayette	600	Athol	110
Muncie	175	Lake Charles	250	***Attleboro	200
Northwest Ind.-Calumet		Monroe	550	Beverly (also incl. in	
Region[N]	2,700	**New Orleans	12,000	Lynn total)	1,000
Richmond	110	*Shreveport	1,200	Boston (Metro.Region)[N]	
***Shelbyville	240	South Central La.[N]			228,000
South Bend[N]	1,900		720	Fall River	1,780
Terre Haute	450			Fitchburg	300
		MAINE		Framingham[N]	10,000
IOWA		Augusta	215	Gardner	100
Ames	200	Bangor	1,300	Gloucester (also incl. in	
Cedar Rapids	300	Biddeford-Saco (incl. in		Lynn total)	400
Council Bluffs (also incl.		So. Maine)		Great Barrington	105
in Omaha total)	150	Brunswick-Bath (incl. in		Greenfield	250
Davenport (incl. in Quad		Southern Maine)		Haverhill	1,500
Cities, Ill.)		***Calais	135	Holyoke	1,100
*Des Moines	3,000	Lewiston-Auburn	500	*Hyannis	1,200
***Dubuque	105	Portland	3,900	Lawrence (incl. in	
Iowa City	750	Rockland	100	Andover total)	
***Mason City	110	Southern Maine (incl.		Leominster	750
***Muscatine	120	Portland)[N]	5,500	Lowell	2,000
**Sioux City	700	Waterville	300	Lynn (incl.Beverly, Pea-	
Waterloo	450			body, and Salem)[N]	
		MARYLAND			19,000
KANSAS		*Annapolis	2,000	New Bedford[N]	2,700
Kansas City (incl. in		**Baltimore	92,000	Newburyport	280
K.C.,Mo.)		Cumberland	265	North Adams (incl. in	
Lawrence	175	Easton Park Area[N]	100	North Berkshire total)	
Manhattan	100	Frederick	400	North Berkshire	675
*Topeka	500	Hagerstown	275	Northampton	700
Wichita[N]	1,000	Harford County	500	Peabody (also incl. in	
		Howard County	7,200	Lynn total)	2,600
KENTUCKY		Montgomery and Prince		Pittsfield (incl.all Berk-	
Covington/Newport		Georges County		shire County)	3,100
(incl. in Cincinnati			99,500	Plymouth	500
total)		Salisbury	400	Salem (also incl. in Lynn	
Lexington[N]	2,000	Silver Spring (incl. in		total)	1,150
*Louisville	9,200	Montgomery County		Southbridge	105
***Paducah	175	total)		Springfield[N]	11,000
				Taunton	1,200

State and City	Jewish Population	State and City	Jewish Population	State and City	Jewish Population
Webster 125		MISSOURI		Bayonne. 4,500	
Worcester[N] 10,000		Columbia. 350		Bergen County[N] 100,000	
		Joplin. 115		Bridgeton. 375	
MICHIGAN		Kansas City Metro.		Camden (incl. in Cherry	
*Ann Arbor 3,000		Area. 22,100		Hill total)	
Battle Creek 245		***Kennett 110		Carteret 300	
Bay City 300		Springfield 230		Cherry Hill[N] . . . 28,000	
***Benton Harbor . . 500		*St. Joseph 325		Edison (incl. in Middle-	
**Detroit. 70,000		**St.Louis 53,500		sex County total)	
*Flint. 2,240				Elizabeth (incl. in Union	
*Grand Rapids . . . 1,500		MONTANA		County)	
***Iron County 160		Billings. 160		Englewood (incl. in Ber-	
***Iron Mountain . . 105		Butte 150		gen County)	
Jackson 375				Essex County[N] .121,000	
*Kalamazoo 1,000		NEBRASKA		Flemington 875	
*Lansing 2,100		Grand Island-Hastings		Gloucester (incl. in	
Marquette County . 175		(incl. in Lincoln total)		Cherry Hill total)	
Mt. Clemens 420		Lincoln 800		Hoboken 350	
Mt. Pleasant 100		Omaha[N]. 6,000		Jersey City. 3,500	
Muskegon 235				Lakewood (incl. in	
*Saginaw 300		NEVADA		Ocean County total)	
***South Haven 100		*Las Vegas 18,000		Middlesex County[N]	
		*Reno 1,200		 39,350	
MINNESOTA				Millville. 240	
***Austin 125		NEW HAMPSHIRE		Monmouth County	
**Duluth. 1,100		Bethlehem 100		 33,600	
***Hibbing 155		Claremont 200		Morris-Sussex counties	
*Minneapolis. . . . 22,000		Concord. 350		(incl. in Essex County)	
Rochester. 240		***Dover. 425		Morristown (incl. in	
**St. Paul 7,500		Hanover-Lebanon . . 360		Morris County)	
***Virginia 100		***Keene. 105		Mt. Holly (also incl. in	
		***Laconia 150		Cherry Hill total). 300	
MISSISSIPPI		Littleton (incl. in		Newark (incl. in Essex	
Biloxi-Gulfport 100		Bethlehem total)		County)	
Clarksdale 160		Manchester[N] 3,000		New Brunswick (incl. in	
Cleveland. 180		Nashua. 450		Middlesex County)	
Greenville 500		Portsmouth 1,000		North Hudson County[N]	
Greenwood 100		Salem (also incl. in An-		 7,000	
Hattiesburg 180		dover, Mass.total). 150		North Jersey[N] . . 28,000	
**Jackson 700				Ocean County. . . 9,500	
Meridian 135		NEW JERSEY		Passaic-Clifton . . 8,000	
***Natchez 140		*Atlantic City (incl. At-		Paterson (incl. in North	
***Vicksburg. 260		lantic County). 15,800		Jersey)	

State and City	Jewish Population
Perth Amboy (incl. in Middlesex County)	
Plainfield (incl. in Union County)	
Princeton	2,600
Salem	230
Somerset County[N]	4,500
Somerville (incl. in Somerset County)	
Toms River (incl. in Ocean County)	
Trenton[N]	8,500
Union County[N]	32,000
Vineland[N]	2,450
Wildwood	425
Willingboro (incl. in Cherry Hill total)	

NEW MEXICO

State and City	Jewish Population
*Albuquerque	4,000
Las Cruces	100
Los Alamos	100
Santa Fe	450

NEW YORK

State and City	Jewish Population
*Albany	12,000
Amenia	140
Amsterdam	595
Auburn	315
***Batavia	165
Beacon (also incl. in Dutchess County total)	315
Binghamton (incl. all Broome County)	3,000
Brewster (also incl. in Danbury, Conn.)	300
*Buffalo	18,500
Canandaigua	135
Catskill	200
***Corning	125
Cortland	440
Dunkirk	150
Ellenville	1,450

State and City	Jewish Population
Elmira[N]	1,100
Geneva	300
Glens Falls[N]	800
Gloversville	535
Herkimer	185
Highland Falls (incl. in Newburgh total)	105
Hudson	470
Ithaca	1,000
Jamestown	185
Kingston[N]	4,000
Lake George (incl. in Glens Falls total)	
Liberty (also incl. in Sullivan County total)	2,100
***Massena	140
Monroe (incl. in Newburgh-Middletown total)	
Monticello (also incl. in Sullivan County total)	2,400
Mountaindale	150
New York City Metro. Area[N]	1,742,500
New Paltz	150
Newark	220
Newburgh-Middletown	8,950
Niagara Falls	550
Norwich	120
Olean	140
Oneonta	175
Oswego	100
Pawling	105
Plattsburg	275
Port Jervis (also incl. in Newburgh total)	560
Potsdam	175
*Poughkeepsie	4,900
**Rochester	19,600
Rockland County	60,000
Rome	205

State and City	Jewish Population
Saratoga Springs	500
**Schenectady	5,400
***Sharon Springs	165
South Fallsburg (also incl. in Sullivan County total)	1,100
Sullivan County	7,425
Syracuse[N]	9,000
Troy area	900
Utica[N]	2,000
Walden (incl. in Newburgh-Middletown)	
Watertown	250

NORTH CAROLINA

State and City	Jewish Population
Asheville[N]	2,100
**Chapel Hill-Durham	2,400
Charlotte[N]	4,000
*Fayetteville	500
Gastonia	220
Goldsboro	120
*Greensboro	2,500
Greenville	300
Hendersonville	105
High Point (incl. in Greensboro)	
Raleigh	1,375
***Rocky Mount	110
Whiteville Zone[N]	160
Wilmington	500
Winston-Salem	300

NORTH DAKOTA

State and City	Jewish Population
Fargo	500
Grand Forks	100

OHIO

State and City	Jewish Population
**Akron	6,000
Athens	100
Bowling Green (also incl. in Toledo total)	120
**Canton	2,500

State and City	Jewish Population
Cincinnati[N]	22,000
**Cleveland	70,000
*Columbus	15,000
**Dayton	6,000
East Liverpool	300
Elyria	275
Hamilton	560
Lima	165
Lorain	1,000
Mansfield	600
Marion	150
Middletown	140
***New Philadelphia	140
**Newark	105
Piqua	120
Portsmouth	120
Sandusky	150
Springfield	340
*Steubenville	200
Toledo[N]	6,300
Warren (also incl. in Youngstown total)	500
Wooster	200
Youngstown[N]	5,000
***Zanesville	350

OKLAHOMA

State and City	Jewish Population
***Muskogee	120
**Oklahoma City	2,300
*Tulsa	2,900

OREGON

State and City	Jewish Population
Corvallis	240
Eugene	1,500
Portland	8,950
***Salem	200

PENNSYLVANIA

State and City	Jewish Population
Aliquippa (also incl. in Pittsburgh total)	400
Allentown	4,980
*Altoona	580
Ambridge (also incl. in Pittsburgh total)	250
Beaver Falls	350
Bethlehem	960
Brownsville	150
Butler	300
***Carbon County	125
Chambersburg	340
Chester (incl. in Phila. total)	
Chester County	3,400
Coatesville (also incl. in Chester County total)	305
Connellsville	110
Delaware Valley (Lower Bucks County)[N]	14,500
Donora (also incl. in Pittsburgh total)	100
Easton	1,300
Ellwood City	110
*Erie	800
Farrell (also incl. in Youngstown, Ohio total)	150
Greensburg (also incl. in Pittsburgh total)	300
**Harrisburg	6,500
Hazleton area	430
Homestead	300
Indiana	135
Johnstown	490
***Kittanning	175
*Lancaster	2,100
Lebanon	425
Lewisburg	125
Lock Haven	140
McKeesport (also incl. in Pittsburgh total)	2,000
Monessen (also incl. in Pittsburgh total)	100
Mt. Pleasant	120
New Castle	400
New Kensington	560
Norristown (incl. in Philadelphia total)	
North Penn	200
Oil City	165
Oxford-Kennett Square	180
Philadelphia area[N]	240,000
Phoenixville (also incl. in Phila. total)	340
Pittsburgh[N]	45,000
Pottstown	700
Pottsville	500
*Reading	2,800
***Sayre	100
*Scranton	3,300
Sharon (also incl. in Youngstown, Ohio total)	330
***Shenandoah	230
State College	450
Stroudsburgh	410
Tamaqua (incl. in Hazleton total)	
Uniontown	390
Upper Beaver County	500
Washington (incl. in Pittsburgh)	
Wayne County	210
West Chester (also incl. in Chester County)	300
Wilkes-Barre[N]	4,000
Williamsport	415
York	1,700

RHODE ISLAND

State and City	Jewish Population
Providence (incl. rest of state)	17,500

SOUTH CAROLINA

State and City	Jewish Population
Aiken	100
*Charleston	3,500
**Columbia	2,000

State and City	Jewish Population	State and City	Jewish Population	State and City	Jewish Population
Florence	350	Lufkin (incl. in Longview total)		Martinsville	135
Greenville	600	Marshall (incl. in Longview total)		Newport News (incl. Hampton)[N]	2,575
***Orangeburg County	105	McAllen	295	Norfolk (incl. Virginia Beach)	12,100
Rock Hill (incl. in Charlotte total)		Odessa-Midland	150	Petersburg	740
Spartanburg	295	Port Arthur	260	Portsmouth-Suffolk (also incl. in Norfolk total)	1,100
Sumter	190	*San Antonio	9,000	Radford (incl. in Blacksburg total)	
		Texarkana	100	Richmond[N]	8,000
SOUTH DAKOTA		Tyler	450	***Roanoke	710
Sioux Falls	125	Waco[N]	500	Williamsburg (incl. in Newport News total)	
		Wharton	170	Winchester	110
TENNESSEE		Wichita Falls	260		
Bristol (incl. in Johnson City total)				WASHINGTON	
Chattanaooga	2,000	UTAH		Bellingham	120
Jackson	120	Ogden	100	Longview-Kelso (incl. in Portland, Ore. total)	
Johnson City	210	*Salt Lake City	2,400	***Olympia	145
Kingsport (incl. in Johnson City total)				Pullman (incl. in Moscow, Idaho total)	
Knoxville	1,350	VERMONT		Seattle[N]	19,500
Memphis	10,000	Bennington	120	Spokane	1,000
Nashville	5,120	Brattleboro	150	Tacoma	750
Oak Ridge	240	Burlington	1,800	Tri Cities[N]	240
		Montpelier-Barre	500		
TEXAS		Rutland	450	WEST VIRGINIA	
Amarillo	300	St. Johnsbury	100	Bluefield-Princeton	250
*Austin	4,000			*Charleston	1,025
Baytown	300	VIRGINIA		Clarksburg	205
***Beaumont	400	Alexandria (incl. Falls Church, Arlington County & Fairfax County)	33,550	Fairmont	100
Brownsville	160			Huntington area[N]	380
College Station	400	Arlington (incl. in Alexandria)		Morgantown	200
*Corpus Christi	1,400	Blacksburg	300	Parkersburg	155
**Dallas	23,000	Charlottesville	800	Weirton	150
De Witt County[N]	150	Chesapeake (incl. in Norfolk total)		Wheeling	650
El Paso	4,800	Danville	180		
*Ft. Worth	3,600	Fredericksburg	140	WISCONSIN	
Galveston	800	Hampton (incl. in Newport News)		Appleton	250
**Houston	42,000	***Harrisonburg	115	Beloit	120
Kilgore (incl. in Longview total)		***Hopewell	140	Eau Clair	120
Laredo	420	Lynchburg	275		
Longview	265				
Lubbock	350				

State and City	Jewish Population	State and City	Jewish Population	State and City	Jewish Population
Fond du Lac	100	Oshkosh	150	Waukesha (incl. in Milwaukee)	
***Green Bay	280	*Racine	375	Wausau	155
*Kenosha	200	Sheboygan	250		
*Madison	4,500	Superior (also incl. in		WYOMING	
Manitowoc	115	Duluth, Minn. total)		Cheyenne	255
Milwaukee[N]	23,900		165		

[N]See Notes below
*Includes entire county
**Includes all of 2 counties
***Figure not updated

Notes

ARKANSAS

Southeast Arkansas–towns in Chicot, Desha, and Drew counties.

CALIFORNIA

Long Beach–includes in L.A. County, Long Beach, Signal Hill, Cerritos, Lakewood, Rosmoor, and Hawaiian Gardens. Includes in Orange County, Los Alamitos, Cypress, Seal Beach, and Huntington Harbor.

Palm Springs–includes Desert Hot Springs, Cathedral City, Palm Desert, and Rancho Mirage.

Pomona Valley–includes Alta Loma, Chino, Claremont, Cucamonga, La Verne, Montclair, Ontario, Pomona, San Dimas, and Upland.

Sacramento–includes Yolo, Placer, El Dorado, and Sacramento counties.

San Francisco–includes San Francisco, Sonoma, Marin, and San Mateo counties and towns of Palo Alto and Los Altos in Santa Clara County.

COLORADO

Denver–includes Adams, Arapahoe, Boulder, Denver, and Jefferson counties.

CONNECTICUT

Bridgeport–includes Monroe, Easton, Trumbull, Fairfield, Bridgeport, Stratford, and part of Milford.

Danbury–includes Danbury, Bethel, New Fairfield, Brookfield, Sherman, Newtown, Redding, Ridgefield, and part of Wilton. Also includes Brewster and Goldens Bridge in New York.

Hartford–includes most of Hartford County and Vernon, Rockville, Ellington, and Tolland in Tolland County.

For a country whose Jewish population estimate of 1984 was not only updated but also revised in the light of improved information, the sign "X" is appended to the accuracy rating.

U.O. SCHMELZ
SERGIO DELLAPERGOLA

TABLE 1. ESTIMATED JEWISH POPULATION, BY CONTINENTS AND MAJOR GEO-
GRAPHICAL REGIONS, 1982 AND 1984

Region	1982 Original	1982 Revised Abs. Nos.	%	1984 Abs. Nos.	%	% Change 1982–84
Diaspora	9,614,300	9,594,300	74.1	9,491,600	73.2	−1.1
Israel	3,374,300	3,349,600	25.9	3,471,700	26.8	+3.6
World	12,988,600	12,943,900	100.0	12,963,300	100.0	+0.2
America, Total	6,477,700	6,477,600	50.1	6,469,000	49.9	−1.3
North[a]	6,013,000	6,015,000	46.5	6,015,000	46.4	—
Central	46,800	46,800	0.4	47,300	0.4	+1.1
South	417,900	415,800	3.2	406,700	3.1	−2.2
Europe, Total	2,842,700	2,825,100	21.8	2,758,600	21.3	−2.6
West	1,070,900	1,053,300	8.1	1,048,900	8.1	−1.0
East & Balkans[b]	1,771,800	1,771,800	13.7	1,709,700	13.2	−3.5
Asia, Total	3,417,200	3,392,500	26.2	3,509,300	27.1	+3.4
Israel	3,374,300	3,349,600	25.9	3,471,700	26.8	+3.6
Rest[b]	42,900	42,900	0.3	37,600	0.3	−12.4
Africa, Total	172,000	169,700	1.3	147,400	1.1	−13.3
North	21,250	19,950	0.2	16,700	0.1	−17.5
South	120,250	119,250	0.9	119,100	0.9	−0.1
Rest[c]	30,500	30,500	0.2	11,600	0.1	−62.0
Oceania	79,000	79,000	0.6	79,000	0.6	—

a U.S.A. and Canada.
b The Asian territories of USSR and Turkey are included in "East Europe and Balkans."
c Including Ethiopia.

Update 1991

They're Coming Home People, Get Ready, There's a Train A-Coming

In October of 1986, thirty-eight of us did a Jericho March around the Kremlin, believing God to break the strongholds binding the Jewish people in the USSR. In that year only about 1,000 Jews had been released from the USSR. A few days after our Jericho March in 1986, the Kremlin agreed to release 12,000 Jews. Every year since then the Lord has had us take another Jericho walk around the Kremlin. In 1988, 16,000 were released. The number rose to 70,000 in 1989 and over 200,000 were released in 1990. We just completed our sixth march during Passover 1991, and we are planning to do our seventh march, led by seven trumpeters, next Passover. The exodus of which Jeremiah prophesied 3,000 years ago (Jeremiah 16:14-16) is happening.

During our 1987 trip a group of watchmen did a Jericho March around the atheist museum in Leningrad, trusting God to break the walls of communism. In 1990, the communists tore the name "atheism" off the museum and are now considering closing it completely and giving it back to the church. (It was a cathedral before the 1907 Bolshevik Revolution.)

Over Passover of 1989, twenty-eight of us went to Russia to pray and work as "fishers" to bring the Jewish people home. God had spoken to me to help mobilize "fishers" to go to Russia. He'd burned on my heart the words of Jeremiah 16:16: "Behold, now I send for many fishers." This Scripture did not apply to the exodus from Egypt or the partial return from Babylon, but it is referring to today. He told me a few fishers had gone forth, but now He is calling for many to go to Russia and throughout all the nations where there are Jewish people, to warn them and help bring them home.

In 1990 we took our fifth mission to Moscow. Eighty of us, including 28 from the International Christian Embassy, went to Moscow, Leningrad, Odessa and Kiev to pray and conduct a concert tour calling and singing the Jewish people home to Israel.

In the last couple of years more copies of *Let My People Go* have gone out in Russian than in English. Russian Jewish leaders are now requesting fifty thousand copies to be distributed in the USSR (a third printing). According to these Jewish leaders, many are opting to come to Israel as a result of reading this book. One of these leaders recently told me that the Facism now emerging in the USSR resembles the atmosphere at the turn of the century when pogroms broke out in 75 Russian cities and two million Jewish people fled to America. He believes this rising Russian nationalism is similar to that of the Nazi rule in Germany and Poland. Russian nationalism (pamyat) is the major anti-Semitic movement in Russia.

While anti-Semitism is breaking out very rapidly in the USSR, it has also been growing in the United States over the last five years. We need to realize that the hunters (anti-Semites) are not only arising in Russia, but also in the west. The time of the fishers (Zionists, those helping and encouraging the Jews to return) is now, and the time of the hunters is at hand. The Jewish people have precious little time to escape from Russia and other nations before God allows more severe circumstances to push them homeward. The fishers must pray, warn, and help so as many as possible can come home in this time of God's grace, before His fuller judgments are released on the Gentile nations!

Let My People Go, released from printing in December of 1987, is calling His people home, not only from Russia, but from the west as well. In America there will be an increase in economic problems that could unleash an anti-Semitism that people thought was impossible. An economic revival is emerging in Europe and Japan but America has peaked and is declining. The Jewish people must return to Israel soon in order to avoid being forced to return as refugees or being caught in the potential holocaust coming to the Gentile nation of America.

Dimitri Dudiman, a prophet from the underground church in Romania, had a vision of New York, Los Angeles, and Miami being destroyed by nuclear missiles. If this happened, four million Jewish people could get caught in a holocaust meant for a Gentile nation and all because they didn't follow the 700 verses in the Tenach calling them home to Israel.

The hour is later than we think. In 1987, as I was driving into New York City, I saw in the spirit many "cities of refuge" as Jewish people were fleeing the city. God gave me Isaiah 60:22 which says that in His time, God will do this very swiftly. The swiftness of the changes in Eastern Europe and in the USSR is a foreshadowing of the swiftness of the changes that could come in the west.

One day when I was praying I saw a vision of a train taking off. The locomotive was the Lord leading the exodus from the USSR, bringing them from the "land of the north" (Jeremiah 16:14). The attached cars represented the Jewish people from all the other cities and nations, immediately following the locomotive. It is time for the Jewish people to get on the train coming out of Russia, but also for them to get on the cars from New York, Los Angeles, Miami, Paris, Buenos Aires, London, Capetown, Toronto, etc. This train is bringing His people home to Israel. Israel will have her problems in the days ahead, but consider the following Scripture:

"And fear not, O Jacob, My servant, declares the Lord, And do not be dismayed, O Israel, for behold I will save you from afar, And your offspring from the land of their captivity. And Jacob shall return, and shall be quiet and at ease, And no one shall make him afraid. For though

I completely destroy the nations to where my people have been scattered. I will not completely destroy you. For I am with you, declares the Lord, to save you; For I will not destroy you completely, But I will chasten you justly, And will by no means leave you unpunished."

As I was talking to a Russian Jew in Moscow, Gad gave me this metaphor: America is like a rose fully blossomed and turning dark, but Israel is like a rose just beginning to bud, to blossom. Just prior to the writing of this third edition, all the Jews were released from Albania in a few days and 95% of the Jews from Ethiopia within thirty-six hours. I talked to an Orthodox Rabbi from New York on my last plane trip to the USA. I asked him if he planned to make aliyah in the future, he said that the Orthodox are planning a massive aliyah within the next few years from New York. Many Jewish people who believe the Bible are now turning their eyes toward Jerusalem and planning their aliyah.

God is now bringing them home from the north, south, east and west.

In 1987, preceding Israel's fortieth birthday, our House of Prayer was born in Jerusalem. Watchmen have come to our Jerusalem House of Prayer for all Nations from over fifty countries, basing their prayers on Isaiah 56:6-8:

"Also the foreigners who join themselves to the Lord, to minister to Him, and to love the name of the Lord to be His servants, every one who keeps from profaning the Sabbath, and holds fast to My covenant; Even those will I bring to My holy mountain and give them joy in My house of prayer. Their burnt offerings and their sacrifices will be accepted on My altar; For My house will be called a house of prayer for all the peoples. The Lord God who gathers the dispersed of Israel, declares, Yet others I will gather to them, besides those already gathered."

(We encourage watchmen and those who want to pray about aliyah to join us in Jerusalem. See the last page of the book for more information.)

Over the past few years, congregations in Israel and abroad have kept a continual fast 24 hours a day, believing God to break the strongholds and bring His people home. God has heard our prayers and is answering.

The future of the Jewish people is in Israel. God's truth is marching onward toward Zion. All roads lead to Jerusalem. People get ready, there's a train a-coming, picking up passengers from coast to coast and continent to continent. This last return will bring Messiah, salvation and peace to Jerusalem. It's later than it's ever been before. Don't miss the train! Get on board!

For a video on the exodus from Russia and the USA or extra copies of this book to give to other Jewish people, please see the form on the following page.

Four Ways You Can Help

1. Become a distributor of *Let My People Go* in your area. For a donation of $120 or more, postage included, receive a box of fifty books. Retail value of books is $300. You can give them to Jewish people in your area or sell them to individuals, churches, bookstores, etc. Individual copies are available in bookstores for $5.95.

> We are believing God for 1,000 distributors throughout the U.S.A. in every Jewish community of over fifty Jewish people! Be God's representative in your area. Send for your box today!

2. Lead or join a team from your area to participate in a 24-hour praise and prayer watch in Jerusalem House of Prayer for All Nations in Israel. Send for more information.

3. Begin a 24-hour prayer watch in your city, state or nation, based on Isaiah 62:6-7 and Isaiah 56:4-8, praying for the peace of Jerusalem and the homecoming of the Jewish people to Israel and to God and the salvation of the Gentiles and abolition of abortion.

4. Financially help this ministry to be able to establish 24-hour houses of prayer in Jerusalem and all nations of the world and states in the U.S.A.

If you are interested in receiving books or other information about our ministry, please write:

Jerusalem House of Prayer for
  All Nations
P.O. Box 31393
Jerusalem 91313 Israel
(If you live outside U.S.A.)

Washington National House
  of Prayer
117 Second Street, N.E. #1
Washington, DC 20002
(If you live in the U.S.A.)

Make all checks payable to Progressive Vision International.

Name _____

Address_____

_____

Telephone _____

(   ) Please send me _____ boxes of 50 books for a donation of $120 or more per box.

(   ) I am interested in coming as an individual or bringing a team to Jerusalem House of Prayer for All Nations. Please send more information.

(   ) I am interested in starting a 24-hour prayer watch in my city, state or nation. Please send more information.

(   ) Enclosed is a gift of $_____ to help establish 24-hour Houses of Prayer in Jerusalem and in nations worldwide.

TEAR OUT AND MAIL